Tailoring

Tailoring

Dressmaking.

Showroom.

Reception and Secretary.

Design and Direction.

Caretaker.

Stockroom

Kenneth King

Hardy Amies Ltd,
14 Savile Row,
London.
W. 1.

Hardy Amies

Hardy Amies

Michael Pick

ACC Editions

DEDICATION

To
Eiji Takahatake

Admired by Sir Hardy Amies
and the author

With love and grateful good wishes

———————————————————

© 2012 Michael Pick
World copyright reserved

ISBN 978 1 85149 675 4

The right of Michael Pick to be identified as the author of this work has
been asserted by him in accordance with the Copyright, Designs and
Patents Act 1988

British Library CIP Data
A catalogue record for this book
is available from the British Library

The paper used within this publication is FSC certified and from
sustainable resources

Printed in Slovenia
Published in England by ACC Editions a division of
the Antique Collectors' Club Ltd., Woodbridge, Suffolk IP12 4SD

CONTENTS

Forewords

Sir Hardy Amies was one of the most famous fashion names to come out of Britain in the mid-twentieth century. He dressed society's most beautiful women and many men too. Arguably the best dressed man of his generation, he was a stickler for correct form in everything from dressing for tennis to addressing the aristocracy. He was a self-confessed snob but great fun with it: talented, amusing and excellent company.
He was a good colleague.

Anna Harvey (Vice President and Editorial Director, Condé Nast Publications)

I first met Hardy Amies nearly thirty years ago, at a lunch-party one Sunday while staying with friends in Gloucestershire. Hardy enchanted me with with his high spirits and his wickedly funny stories, and he, recognising I suppose an appreciative audience, soon afterwards invited me to attend a concert with him. From then on we became friends and saw each other regularly. Sometimes he dined at my house, always a slightly nerve-wracking occasion as his standards were high, and I often spent a weekend with him in the country. His friendship was not only a pleasure but an education. I learned the difference between chic and "naff" (a favourite word); about food and how to make the best martini; and, most fascinatingly, about his early life in England, France and Germany, although he would never be drawn on the subject of his remarkable (as we now know) wartime career.

I particularly loved Hardy for his warmth and wit, his generous nature, for his sometimes reckless indiscretion, and for his never-failing enthusiasm and love of life.

Selina Hastings

'You've got to fit in and dispense happiness,' Hardy Amies once confided to my wife, Pat, and he spent his whole life practising this philosophy.

I first met Hardy through Pat at the beginning of our marriage some forty-five years ago and he literally changed our lives by introducing us to homeopathy. He only used this alternative medicine and claimed never to have had a headache.

Certainly his energy was prodigious, playing weekend tennis as well as managing a thriving business all over the world. The son of a court dressmaker, he learned early on the importance of 'the fit'. He exemplified English style, not just in his own wardrobe and designs but in his private passions.

Weekends were for the country in the houses that he loved. He converted an old school house in Oxfordshire where we spent time with other fortunate guests. That was how we met his close colleague and collaborator, the delightful, talented Ken Fleetwood. Hardy enjoyed many other passions such as gardening, breakfast marmalade made by his cook, and opera. We were thrilled to meet the great Joan Sutherland in his elegant London house at a dinner party, another passion.

As traditional as he was, he also embraced the new world and its fashions and styles. He had a modern apartment in New York which he kindly let us rent. Indeed, generosity was a byword for him. He considered that life should be enjoyed and he passed on this enjoyment to others. An all round life-enhancer, there was nothing pompous or straight-laced about him. Never was a knighthood more thoroughly deserved or enjoyed. It was a privilege to have known Sir Hardy.

Michael York
July 2012
(Photo courtesy Pat York)

INTRODUCTION

To many people, he was 'Hardly Amiable', a chilly, supercilious snob with a dead-pan expression and a gaze that could freeze the joy out of a conversation. To many others, he was a gregarious, urbane companion with a fund of witty observations and stories covering a wide range of interests and a sympathetic friend. Sir Hardy Amies was sympathetic to those he felt deserving of his kindness, irrespective of their background, and unkind to those he felt had no substance, empty characters, often masked by pretentious behaviour. Ever the astute observer of human nature, he could spot an imposter from across the room. If he gained a reputation for loving a duchess, it was not simply that the Essex boy forever inside him wanted to scale the social ladder, he was wholeheartedly interested in most aspects of British history and what her family represented – business possibilities apart. For business was never far from his thoughts, as he kept abreast of fashion's serpentine progress over seven decades. Many other designers faltered and failed; Sir Hardy survived to become yet another headline, 'Hardy Perennial'.

Amies began his unplanned life in fashion during the mid-1930s, when London was already perceived from across the Atlantic by the all-important American store buyers as a viable fashion centre with a different perspective from that of Paris and one of interest to American women. This was largely the result of pioneering work by Norman Hartnell and it obsessed Amies, as much as it did French designers, when American store buyers began to visit the London collections, most often before the French. After his first success in 1935, Amies made sure that he had a lucrative American market for the rest of his working life.

When he suggested to me that I write this book, I was quizzing him about Norman Hartnell. 'Normie was a soppy old queen,' he paused, 'I am a bitchy old queen. That's the difference.' Of course, I knew that this was only an amusingly glib line, although there was some truth in it. As it turned out he admired Hartnell, as he did Cecil Beaton, whom he summed up, 'Cecil was an unhappy queen and I have been a happy queen'. His positive attitude to life was most apparent. We met at infrequent intervals, initially at 14 Savile Row, Buck's Club, and then in his Cornwall Gardens flat, where we would wait until Peter Hope-Lumley, his press officer of some five decades and chaperone against wild utterances, fell asleep on the sofa. I wondered why he should want another book about his life, having already written two autobiographies. The eyes glittered, 'I have so much more to tell!' He did, and was fascinating about his young years in Germany, revelling in salacious details, as he re-lived his years. I began to feel that I was becoming a mixture of Father Confessor and psychiatrist, the effect spoilt by Peter waking with a grunt. Conversation became more sedate.

Lunches, dinners in my house and with our mutual friend Kenneth Partridge also followed, a few parties too, one at Claridges with Ken Fleetwood and later Hardy's ninetieth birthday party in Savile Row, where I met his sister Rosemary. I interviewed him for Judy Price's New York glossy magazine *Avenue* and we talked more intently about his life and career, then fate overtook both of us. My career path and family commitments all changed radically and as he became infirm and resident less and less in London, the idea of an Amies biography faded and Hartnell's took precedence.

Readers of this book will do well to consult Hardy Amies' autobiography of 1954, *Just So Far*. Although often sparse on detailed fact and events, it gives not only his own voice when at the height of his powers, but also delineates the making and maintaining of a viable London couture house of the period. Amies already saw the future for all such London businesses in 1954. He never shirked from saying that Paris led fashion and London followed, not as a second-rate follower, but one which excelled in a British way giving a British twist to what France, and especially Dior, was innovating. The lack of a sufficient number of adequately trained workers and more positive government backing were both indicted by Amies as reasons for London's subsidiary status, not lack of design talent.

By 1985, the date of his second volume, *Still Here*, and the title says it all, Amies was already a lively seventy-six and had been in the business for half a century. Much of that book paraphrases *Just So Far*, but the years after 1954 make interesting reading, not least in designing for the Queen or becoming a 'Living Label' , as he headed one chapter. Often meandering and confusing in its structure and chronology, apparently dictated not written, the autobiography is indispensable in so forcefully reproducing the voice of the author.

The greatest difficulty in writing a full biography lies in the same problem, which must have affected Hardy Amies in his own writing: he kept almost nothing of his past. Letters and papers were destroyed as he went along. Together with Ken Fleetwood, a loyal younger companion from 1952 until his own death in 1995, they also made a bonfire of almost all the design sketches not relating to their work for the Queen. Luckily the Amies pocket and desk diaries he clearly consulted largely remain intact, but they only begin in 1940. Had his sister Rosemary not kept photographs and albums, there would be very little personal memorabilia, which has led to much impatient detective work and thankful delving into the Hardy Amies in-house press books. Perhaps it is indicative that the most complete documentary record of his life is found in his mostly preserved bank statements from his days at Lachasse onwards.

Amies was never reticent in giving his opinions. He first appeared in the 1930s on the embryonic BBC television, was a regular broadcaster from then on and even participated in the long-running radio show *Any*

Questions. Until the end, he was a master self-publicist, always delighted to give an interview or pen an article or book review – his March 1957 scathing dissection of 'Mrs Fraser's translation from the French' of Christian Dior's 1956 autobiography might have made the young Lady Antonia Fraser think twice about translating anything again, if she ever read it in *Truth* magazine. The review is also notable for his comment, 'His chapter on London I find a little too obsequious. Although it is relieved by some slightly malicious digs at the clothes of certain grand ladies. It is difficult to make any Frenchman, much less M. Dior, understand that English ladies never will consider clothes worthy of close attention or great expenditure.' Even before he received his KCVO, Amies could not refrain from commenting on his designs for the Queen, but was never less than totally loyal and devoted to her, no matter what odd comments might occasionally be uttered.

If none of this sounds particularly heart-warming, Amies was not one to flaunt or express the embarrassing look-at-me open emotion so often found in Britan today. He came of tough stock, emotions were controlled with a stiff upper lip and, in his case, usually a deadpan expression. He swiftly matured through the hard times following the First World War, in his turn having to take part in the Second, during which he was partly responsible for sending young SOE agents to an uncertain future, quite often their capture, torture and death. He clearly liked being with people and delighted in the company of younger generations. Geoffrey Angold, a former employee, vividly remembers a party held in his own flat during October 1971, which included guests of various nationalities. Amies effortlessly charmed them all without any pretension, speaking to them in their own languages. He also had a great sense of humour, as his clerihews prove, and many of his favourite films were comedies. He loved annual trips with friends to pantomimes for years, until they became too tv-star orientated for his taste, and laughed at the comedy of Kenneth Williams, Peter Cook and Fenella Fielding in the 1959 revue, *Pieces of Eight* – he went with guests twice.

Perhaps Amies' ceaseless frenetic round of developing new aspects of his business, constant travel, passion for opera, music, entertainment, sporting activities, socialising, reading and forever learning about something new, was a heightened result of his traumatic wartime existence. He never spoke much about it, but like the aspiring Essex school boy, it was a part of him that was locked up inside, but not revisited, whereas he often returned to his Brentwood School roots. He was delighted that the Hardy Amies Design Centre was named after him, when opened there in 1999, his ninetieth year, and a decade after the Queen invested him with the KCVO. He was always happy to point out that this was not an honour from the government, but a personal gift from the Queen. This book will hopefully demonstrate how well deserved that honour was, when bestowed on an Englishman of so many talents.

CHAPTER ONE

THE HARDY PERENNIAL

Hardy Amies

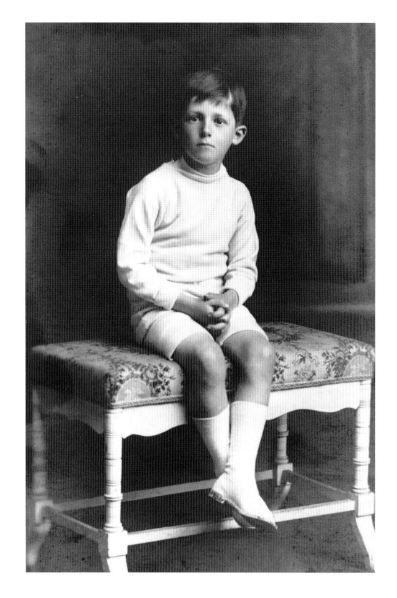

Above left: Edwin Hardy Amies aged six in 1915, when he attended Latymer Upper School, whilst his father was still with the British Army in France.

Above right: Mother and son at home during the First World War, circa 1915.

Below: Hardy on the beach at Southwold, summer 1921. Holidays were invariably spent with his family at the more bracing English seaside resorts.

Hardy Amies considered that dress designers were born, not made. In retrospect, he viewed his career as a natural progression of latent talents, primarily stemming from his childhood exposure to his mother's work as a saleswoman with successful Edwardian Court Dressmakers, which began with 'Madame Machinka' at 36 Dover Street in Mayfair, London. In 1996 he amended this decades–long official version to state that she had begun her working life as a seamstress, which explains her later role in sewing costumes for a pageant and her full comprehension of the workings of a couture business, as explained to Hardy from an early age. (*Still Here; Just So Far; Daily Mail* 16 November 1996)

In retrospect, he was a most unlikely candidate for his future success as a designer, a career that ultimately began by chance. After leaving Brentwood School in 1927 he learned about the world and business in

Previous page: Hardy Amies and companions at the 1931 Pageant of Essex, in aid of the King George Hospital, Ilford. Hardy's parents were prominent supporters of the hospital, and his mother Mary created the costumes for two scenes.

France and Germany, returning to England in 1930, but not until 1934 did he begin work at the dressmakers Lachasse. There is every reason to assume that his talent as a dress designer was something with which he was born, and that experience then contributed to his success.

In his writing and speech, Amies stressed the influence of his mother's short career on his future success, mainly through the contacts she made and then nurtured after she ceased working around 1912. This combination of immediate family influences, combined with his ancestry to make him an effective designer and businessman. They also contributed to his capabilities as a wartime officer, as head of the Belgian T–Section of the Special Operations Executive (SOE), a remarkable appointment attesting to exceptional organisational and inspirational skills, coupled with great diplomacy and powers of invention. A relatively brief interlude in a long life of achievements, this intense experience caused him anguish at the time, later suppressed, it returned at the end of his life to haunt him.

Edwin Hardy Amies, christened with his paternal grandfather's Christian name and the surname of his maternal grandfather, was born on 17 July 1909 in Delaware Mansions, Elgin Avenue, Maida Vale. At that time it was a quiet leafy area, only fifteen minutes by road from fashionable Mayfair where his mother Mary worked, and his father's offices near The Mall. Elgin Avenue is the longest tree-lined avenue (or *boulevard*) in London, and it is fitting that Hardy had the lifelong air of a sophisticated Edwardian *boulevardier*, largely gained in his late teens when working in France and Germany. Writing in 1954, Hardy remembered the white paint, yellow walls and lace curtains of the Elgin Avenue flat, with memories of Mademoiselle Louise Probet-Piolat, one of his mother's colleagues, known as Aunt Louie, who lived nearby and in 1933 played a major role in his choice of career.

His parents were hard-working aspirational Victorians, born in the English countryside who migrated to London to seek work, as their family circumstances dwindled. According to Hardy, his father Herbert William Amies (born 1880) first saw Mary Hardy (born 1883) on Bond Street looking into the window of Chappell's music shop as she left work and he followed her to the Bayswater bus. His persistence paid off, and they were eventually married at St Bartholomew's Church in the rather down-at-heel neighbourhood of Camberwell in 1906. On the marriage certificate, his profession is given as 'Surveyor of Kensington' and Mary Hardy as a 'spinster of no occupation'. Her father Thomas's profession that of coach-builder, a variant on Hardy's version, but confirming Hardy Amies' 1954 statement that he was born a Cockney.

Right, above: *Hardy with his baby sister Rosemary in the garden at Alperton in 1916. Known in the family by her second name, Peggy, she and Hardy remained extremely close throughout their lives.*

Right: *A studio shot of Hardy, taken at the same time, the tailored double-breasted coat with wide revers and velvet collar is a sign of things to come. The coat is attributed to a tailor in Miss Gray's workrooms, his mother's last employer in 1915.*

The Hardy Perennial

Hardy aged fifteen in 1924 as Mrs Malaprop, front row, second from right, in the Brentwood School production of Sheridan's The Rivals.

Hardy aged fourteen as the Earl of Worcester, front row, far right, December 1923. His performances were the highlight of his year, as he showed no interest in the sports fields, but did win his only cup – for dancing the Charleston.

By his own account, both of his parents were products of financially turbulent Victorian families, familiar to modern readers in the novels of Charles Dickens. His maternal grandmother Rose was born into a family of shopkeepers in Windsor, and married Thomas Hardy, heir to the ailing Griffin Hotel in Kingston-on-Thames, which was eventually sold, the proceeds funding a glass and china shop in Dorking, Surrey. Rose was mother of five children, but the marriage was unsuccesful, and she bade farewell to her husband Thomas, who sailed with her full co-operation for a new life in Canada, leaving her with an unborn sixth child. Sadly Rose's china shop did not prosper and was sold, and she then bought a lodging house in Bayswater, London. On Herbert and Mary's marriage certificate, Edwin Amies and Rose Hardy were the witnesses, Thomas had long since gone. As a middle child, Hardy Amies' mother Mary had an uncomfortable upbringing, but her considerable personality and charm, remarked on in the local newspaper after her death in August 1938, enabled her to become a highly-regarded saleswoman with a number of the better-situated Court Dressmakers, one of several hundred such businesses then in existence.

The term 'Court Dressmaker' dwindled in the Second World War. It indicated dressmakers specialising in clothes worn by those presented or admitted to the presence of the Sovereign, usually at Buckingham Palace. The client could rely upon such an established business to produce a variety of well-made fashionable clothing of superlative construction appropriate to occasions with a royal presence. With much competition in existence, the saleswoman or *vendeuses* of Court Dressmakers required considerable persuasive skills and charm to retain and satisfy a demanding and fickle clientele. Such attributes were certainly inherited by Hardy Amies.

The Brentwood School Officer Training Corps camp in Belgium, circa 1925. It was Hardy's first trip abroad, soon to be followed by many more.

Above left: *On holiday with his mother, a friend, and Rosemary in Margate, circa 1924. In common with many English schoolchildren until the 1960s, expensive school uniform was usually worn on smarter occasions.*

Above right: *Hardy and Rosemary on Purbeck Island, on his return from Germany in 1930. According to Hardy, 'she had no interest in clothes whatsoever'. The formerly bookish, if extrovert, schoolboy had been energised by the youth culture of Germany and inspired his sister to follow his example.*

Hardy Amies' father Herbert was the son of a provincial Kent manufacturing family, reputedly of French descent. The Victorian firm of Edwin Amies & Sons left family ownership in the 1940s, but existed in Maidstone, Kent until 2009 as mould makers and were 'Dandy Roll' suppliers to the local paper manufacturers. The term amused Hardy, intrigued by his ancestry and history, but there is considerable artistic and mechanical skill involved in creating Dandy Rolls: intricate wire-mesh plates which are embellished with a design forming a watermark in paper as it is pressed onto the wet pulpy mixture nearing the end of the production process. 'Amies Rolls' were good enough for paper used in banking, including the fine Waterlow mark, one of their many pre-First World War commissions. The Amies family epitomised the adage of 'clogs-to-clogs in three generations' and Hardy was bemused by the large ageing household existing in gentility on the outskirts of Maidstone, their coachman being an uncle. Yet, he clearly inherited their industry and aptitude for envisaging mechanical form and construction, combined with artistry.

Herbert Amies had a solid local education at Sutton Valence School and was articled to an architect. Lack of finance meant that he left and joined the offices of the Valuation Department of the London County Council. He was

Left: *Hardy on a quiet English Sunday on the river in the 1920s, in the nearest he then had to a sporting outfit, a school blazer and cricket flannels.*

King George V and Queen Mary visited Becontree in 1923 and 1931, here accompanied by Hardy's father Captain Herbert Amies, the Resident Agent for the London County Council.

later a paid chorister in St Mark's Church, Hamilton Terrace, at the top of Elgin Avenue, instilling in Hardy a lifelong passion for opera, as he heard his father singing at home in the evenings. Around 1912, the family moved to a small terraced house with a garden in the unlikely area of Alperton, now part of Wembley, on the banks of the Grand Union Canal and notorious for the noxious smells from barge-loads of gas-lime and dung, a sewage farm, two rubbish sorting yards and three large piggeries. Alperton had been notorious for brawling workmen with bare-knuckle boxing and even cockfights until cleaned up around 1895 and the subsequent arrival of a railway connection convenient to the West End for both parents.

Typically, Hardy remembered the roses, the black and white tiles to the white-painted front door protected by a black and white striped sun blind,

The Hardy Perennial

Brentwood School became co-educational in stages from 1974 and Hardy Amies redesigned the uniforms in 1995. Thirty years after he left school, the Queen visited in October 1957, wearing an ensemble designed by him and asked that he be present.

but he was only five when he heard from a neighbour of war in August 1914. His sister Rosemary was born on 19 October 1915, whilst their father was in the army in France. This was a significant moment in Hardy's life and they remained extraordinarily close for the rest of their lives, eventually buying houses in the same Oxfordshire village of Langford.

A sharpshooter in the City of London Yeomanry and then a Lance Corporal, Herbert Amies was called up to serve in the Army in 1914, becoming 2ⁿᵈ Lieutenant in the Middlesex Regiment by September 1915, then Acting Captain and finally by May 1917, Adjutant. The London family house was let, and mother and son went to live in various rooms in the Kent countryside, where Herbert was training for active service. Hardy was taken from infant school in Wembley and on returning to Alperton with baby Rosemary, sent to Latymer Upper School in Hammersmith, where he learned of the Armistice in November 1918. Unsurprisingly, their father Herbert had become a stranger to Hardy and Rosemary. She answered the door bell in 1919, calling out 'Mummy, come quickly, there's a man at the door'. 'From then on we were inseparable.' she wrote (*Hardy Amies Langford Archive*).

Herbert returned from the war with organisational skills and the mature determination of the survivor. London County Council appointed him as Resident Agent for one of the largest public housing schemes in the world, set on Essex land between Dagenham and Barking, involving the acquisition of land and construction of small houses and gardens. When Captain Amies moved his family to Gale Street Farm, Rippleside, Barking, the early Victorian farmhouse was surrounded by fields of rhubarb, vegetables and produce for Covent Garden, with carts pulled by Clydesdale horses. Hardy and Rosemary later described how over the next twenty years, the farm became surrounded by a vast swathe of brick, and a late photograph of Herbert in his garden shows the new houses just beyond his hedges.

In his autobiographies, Hardy was remarkably diffident about his father's achievements, representing him as a glorified rent-collector, but an American writer investigating housing conditions in the mid-1930s gave a different impression:

'On our schedule was a visit to Becontree, the mammoth housing development of the London County Council, which provided homes for more than 125,000 people. En route from London, we had driven through the crawling slums of Limehouse, not quite as bad as in Dickens' time, thanks to Becontree, which had absorbed many families from that squalid district.

'Captain Amies, the manager, unfolded his six-feet-four frame and momentarily removed his pipe as his face broke into an expansive smile.

"So you are from the States and interested in housing, eh?" he drawled. "Well, we have plenty of it here.... Let's take the figures first," he suggested. "There are 26,000 houses, 130,000 population, 27 churches, 30 schools, 400 shops, 21 rent offices, 500 acres of parks and open spaces - total cost about 13,000,000 pounds."

Left: *Learning French in the summer of 1927. Hardy, top right, en famille with the Vernet-Barbarroux family in the countryside of Le Vieux Cannet, Le Luc in the Var.*

Below: *The young adult Hardy Amies, far right, in Bendorf-am-Rhein, with his hosts Frau von Claer and family enjoying a typically German Sunday afternoon stroll on the banks of the Rhine in 1929. Jonny Witte is third from right.*

The Hardy Perennial

Early employment in 1928, learning German and business practices with Jonny Witte, then manager, at the Rheinische Wandplatten Fabrik GmbH . Hardy, the young professional in the works office white coat, is standing in the doorway. Witte bought the factory in 1941 and it was a local landmark, surviving war and fires. It was finally demolished in the late 1970s, after Jonny Witte's death.

I was duly impressed by these astronomical figures, which added up to the biggest project of its kind in the world.

"We are only eleven miles from the center of London," Captain Amies continued, "about a half-hour by train. We're a working-class town.... We've tried to get private enterprise to build for upper middle-class people, but they won't because of the bad approach through the industrial, dock, and slum districts of London's East End. In another way, it helps to be a workers' town since factories follow the labor pool. There were practically no industries in this area when we came. Now there are the Ford and Briggs auto-body plants at nearby Dagenham, and many other factories, all because they can get labor right here. A lot of folks used to be clerks in London, but the weekly fare to the city is about eight shillings - a big item in the family budget - so many of them have switched to jobs in this neighborhood."

When we reached the residential area, Laura remarked about the well-clipped hedges that lined all the streets, and asked if the tenants maintain them.

"We look after the sixty miles along the street, but the householders take care of the additional two hundred and twenty miles of hedges that separate the rear gardens," grunted Captain Amies as he mopped his brow.

"Now suppose we stop at a house whose garden won first prize in the area." All was immaculate, and the aproned wife made us feel at home. The rear yard was a profusion of blooming shrubs, flowers, and well-tended grass. But so were the yards of all the neighbors.

No residential building was more than two stories high. The entire estate was dotted with numberless small green plots and playing fields. There was much to see, but we could do little more than sample the tremendous development.

We drove back to London through the vast expanse of slums that still remained. The violent contrast between them and Becontree was a silent but vigorous plea for public housing.'

Adventures of a Slum Fighter, Charles F Palmer
(Tupper and Love, USA, 1955)

This important work of the local council and the LCC was recognised by two visits from King George V and Queen Mary in 1923 and 1931.

The move benefited the Amies family. Mary became absorbed with the local hospital, church and charity work. Hardy continued his education at Brentwood School, founded in 1558 with the motto prized by Hardy for the rest of his life: 'Virtue, Learning, Manners'. Hardy entered the school on 30 April 1920, remaining until 1927. Initially he travelled by train, but unusually pestered his parents until he became a boarder. His lifelong affection for Brentwood resulted in many visits; in 1995 he redesigned the school uniforms, and in 1999 he opened the Hardy Amies Design Centre.

Re-adjustment to life with his imposing father became even more difficult in 1918 with the birth of Wilfred, a Down Syndrome child, never referred to publicly by him or Rosemary, but loved, provided for, visited regularly and given holidays by them until his death. The children of the Amies–Hardy marriage were unusual. Hardy and Rosemary both sought their own sex in close relationships; as she said to some friends: 'The wrong one got the balls'. Had they considered marriage, the thought of a child was difficult, their brother remained at the mental age of ten until his death.

In contrast to his later life, Hardy showed no sporting interests at school. He blossomed under the encouragement of the young English teacher Howard Hayden, becoming an extrovert actor in every school play he could get into, even going behind someone's back to persuade the director he was a better actor. As Jessica in the *The Merchant of Venice* in Spring 1922, 'fault could scarcely be found'. Prophetically, in view of his long career based in playwright Richard Sheridan's former London town-house, he played Mrs Malaprop in *The Rivals* where 'the ladies amusing solecisms were delivered to great effect, and the affectations of an elderly and conceited lady were copied with remarkable fidelity.'

Equally prophetically, Hardy was sent with his school Officer Training Corps unit to a camp in Belgium. By now his extrovert nature was well-established: his 1926 speech day performance as Petruccio from *The Taming of the Shrew* caused an audible comment from a woman in the audience: 'Oh, just look at the great big bully', which underlines his strength of personality. He was a school Praeposter (prefect) and performed a final part as Malvolio in *Twelfth Night*: 'Malvolio did really well....an actor of considerable experience and has proved his ability in a long series of roles.' (Brentwood School archive) During the Second World War,

Above: *Hardy and Jonny relaxing with books. Jonny gave Hardy many books on literature, philosophy and related subjects.*

Below: *Outside a Rhineland hotel, Hardy (left) and Jonny with a friend in typical German countrified clothing, autumn 1929. Hardy is clearly no longer the young adolescent first seen in Bendorf, but a competent businessman with a successful German company.*

The Hardy Perennial

Winter 1929. Invigorated by the sports culture of the period in Germany and encouraged by Jonny (front left), Hardy (sitting right) learnt to ski and continued to do so until the 1960s. This was the beginning of his later passions for tennis and ice-skating, for which he had professional tuition.

Hardy's knowledge of Shakespeare often became the basis of naming missions and agents under his control within the Belgian Section of SOE.

In 1926 Hardy went off to France to improve his language skills. Having sat his School Certificate, he sadly failed the entrance exams for Cambridge University, considering that he had been entered too soon, but by now there were financial constraints at home. His mother looked after the family alone, Wilfred and the future finance of his care had to be considered. As soon as Hardy left school in 1927, Rosemary went as a boarder to Brentwood County High School. 'I wonder if we were ever an emotional family' he wondered. 'Certainly there was no marked display of affection. Even present giving was brought to a minimum and a Christmas present was often a new overcoat or a pair of shoes.' (JSF p.30)

At the suggestion of his English teacher Howard Heyden (and ignoring Hardy's obvious potential as an actor) his father took him to meet the American editor of the *Daily Express*, R. D. Blumenfeld, who advised him

Opposite page: The Rhineland towns and cities are particularly known for their wholehearted enjoyment of 'Karneval' every year with many Shrove Tuesday balls and parties frequently in fancy dress. Hardy and Jonny with friends, 1930.

to learn languages abroad. Hardy duly took up a teaching post at a language school in Antibes in April 1927. He learnt little, but he did renew his acquaintance with his mother's friend 'Aunt Louie', formerly of Elgin Avenue, now living in Nice. She sent him to stay with a family in the countryside, where he expanded his knowledge and then worked for a Parisian carriers and customs agents, contacts of his mother's last dressmaking employer, Miss Gray. He bought books, visited the theatre and grew to love Paris. His mother's friendships came to determine Hardy's life.

These years working abroad constituted Hardy's university education, and in 1928 he set off for Bendorf-am-Rhein, then a picturesque small town near Koblenz, where his Aunt Hardy had discovered an eighteenth-century *Pfarrhaus* (vicarage) where the Pfarrer von Claer took paying language students. Now rebuilt after being heavily destroyed in the war, this idyllic setting was where Hardy blossomed, learning German and experiencing the clash between extreme modernity and traditional German life. Although treated rather condescendingly by the Pfarrer, he discovered music, opera, theatre, wine, good food, sports and literature, as well as his sexuality in a passionate friendship. He also witnessed the departure of the French troops of occupation from Koblenz, and the Weimar Republic crumble. Hardy needed money, and he made the acquaintance of the young manager of the local tile factory, Johann 'Jonny' Witte. In his early thirties, Jonny appointed Hardy as office manager and travelling salesman for the industrial stone or white coloured tiles: Hardy's first recorded design attempts for new tiles were considered hideous.

The death of the German Chancellor Gustav Stresemann and the Wall Street Crash in October 1929 had disastrous consequences for Germany, and in July 1930 on becoming twenty-one, Hardy returned to England, at the behest of his father, ostensibly to become a journalist. His intense friendship with Jonny in the small confines of Bendorf had cooled, it was one in which Hardy learned all he could from an older man and he returned to England.

Rosemary then demonstrated her independent spirit by living with a Jewish family in Berlin on an exchange scheme until 1937. Jonny and the Rheinische Wandplattenfabrik factory survived the war; he bought the factory in 1941 and owned it until 1969. Their friendship was renewed after the war. Hardy and Rosemary visited Bendorf again in 1965 after being present during the State Visit of the Queen to West Germany, and from 1953 Hardy Amies' Visitors' Book records visits by Jonny over the years, until his death in 1973.

Apart from photographs, little exists of Hardy's pre-1940 life, but the books Jonny gave him still survive, and are evidence of an intense intellectual friendship. In October 1928 he gave Hardy a copy of *Erlebnisse der Stille* (Experiences of Quiescence), a new collection of philosophical essays by a follower of Stefan George and Rudolf Steiner, Ernst Bacmeister. This was followed in November 1928 with a copy of Goethe's *Leiden des Jungen Werthers* (The Sorrows of Young Werther) in which he wrote a dedication to Hardy in German, which translates as:

The Pageant of Essex in 1931, with which Hardy's family were involved. Hardy, far right, took part in the pageant on a visit home from his work as a salesman with W. & T. Avery Ltd., weighing-machine manufacturers in Smethwick, Birmingham.

An Introduction: In this book feeling is everything, the last and highest attribute! In short, life! Understanding, intelligence are nothing, absolutely nothing! Our comprehending, understanding, intelligent generation of today smiles in a mocking, uncaring way! It is true - this is in Goethe, but one shrugs it of as a reflection of an age... Achieving a record is now everything. The more women are used by a man, the more a woman can behave in a furtive or veiled manner, the better! That is a record, that is success ! A record, a success which drives one into spiritual death. I wish that a poet would stand up and preach again: feeling is everything! Preach so impressively that you would understand, cold, clever, spiritually dead humanity, which is obsessed by records and the tempo of our times, will hear so that you will reflect on yourself, so that you will weep tears over your lost past. Feel your lost spirituality. Live your lost godly ideals! Only when you feel are you akin to God! Be that, which you are meant to be! Jonny, 28 November 1928.

This dedication sums up the mood and serves as an epitaph to the disintegrating Germany Hardy loved so much; so much so that he next found a post with the Karlsruhe branch of the Birmingham Avery weighing machines company. It was short lived: the company recognised the future, closed their German branches, and Hardy found himself working in their Birmingham office for four years.

CHAPTER TWO

LEARNING AT LACHASSE

Hardy Amies

Learning at Lachasse

On 1 February 1934, Hardy Amies began his new career at Lachasse, a relatively new dressmaker established in 1928 at the heart of fashionable Mayfair. Not yet employed as designer, he was manager of the business, based upon his experience and an interest in fashion. Having left Germany on 1 July 1930 for a visit to his parents, he intended to return after his twenty-first birthday in July to work in their Karlsruhe branch of the British weighing-machine company W. & T. Avery Ltd., utilising his excellent knowledge of french and german.

A combination of the world economic crisis and deteriorating German political situation caused Avery to retrench, so Hardy found himself instead training in the Smethwick headquarters, 'hating the din of the workshops and the petty routine of the large office'. As in Bendorf, he quickly mastered the business and became an adept salesman, scouting for shops and businesses in need of new scales, lugging the heavy machines from door to door, and even winning a silver cigarette box and membership of the firm's 'Hundred Club' for salesmen who had sold more than one hundred machines a month. Soon his target was two hundred scales a month, first in the tough East End of London and latterly in the Oxford area.

Previous page: Hardy Amies the elegant young designer feeling at home, wearing and embowered by swathes of wool at Lachasse in his first year, 1934.

Above: Hardy Amies at Lachasse illustrated in Vogue of October 1936 with the caption 'Nipped in line for day. Backs foremost in interest, fur treated unconventionally – these two points are proven on Lachasse's black cloth coat with Persian lamb and seaming pushing the waistline up the shoulders'. This demonstrates that Amies designs soon made an impact on the fashion circles that counted. (Bouty/Vogue © The Condé Nast Publications Ltd.)

Right: Hardy Amies at Lachasse, an early success with a sleek tailored suit for Lady Mountbatten, who bought 'sports clothes' including this tweed suit of duck-egg blue flecked brown-beige herringbone pattern. The slim skirt and jacket are given ultra-slim lines by the vertical inset panels and the small kick-pleats above the hemline. Circa 1935.

Opposite page: A country suit should also be 'elegant enough to wear for lunch at the Ritz', according to Hardy Amies. The well-bred Lachasse look of the mid-1930s included long detailed skirts, closely-fitted jackets and top-coats, made in the same style with fur trimmings, all worn with neat, wind-proof, small hats. 1936.

By 1933 Hardy had congenial rooms in Birmingham, played tennis and enjoyed concerts, but his greatest pleasure lay in his small open tourer which he drove around the Cotswolds countryside. This sense of idyllic freedom with no cares or responsibilities was later remembered as the happiest time of his life. Had he been posted to Germany, it is inconceivable that he would have remained. Rosemary continued to visit Berlin until 1937, where she provided support to a Jewish family and witnessed increasing fear and repression. On his annual week-long visits to Bendorf up to 1938, Hardy remarked on what he termed 'the Nazification of the Pfarrhaus', even Jonny liking the 'apparent fairness and order of the new regime'. (*JSF* p.69)

Thinking back to his school acting successes, Hardy wrote a play and was encouraged by a producer, who said the play was 'dreadful but that it showed some promise'. (*JSF* p.50) Of this time Hardy wrote , 'No one should be content with what they are doing if they are ambitious or frustrated...keep on your toes...the moment a new door is opened for you, you can decide in a flash if the adventure in the next room would be good for you, and then leap unhesitatingly.' (*JSF* p.52)

Such a moment occurred after a charity dance before Christmas 1933, to which Hardy had been asked by Mrs Shingleton, his mother's friend and former employer at Miss Gray Ltd. Court Dressmakers. Mrs Shingleton and her husband managed three businesses: Miss Gray Ltd. in Brook Street; the couture house Paulette on the Champs Elysées, with its London branch in Berkeley Square; and Lachasse in Farm Street, where the designer was the talented Digby Morton, well-known for elegant women's suits. It says much for Mary Hardy that during the twenty years since she left Miss Gray Ltd., she and Mrs Singleton had remained friends.

Hardy wrote to 'Aunt Louie' in Nice describing in vivid detail Mrs Shingleton's elegance and her dress at the Christmas dance. The letter was then forwarded to Mrs Shingleton who handed it to her husband with the words: 'You ought to get that boy into the business in Digby Morton's place', as Morton was leaving to found his own business. Hardy was interviewed, offered a post with a vague job description at half the salary he had been earning with Avery, and only received a contract as Managing Designer after a year.

He found himself working in a converted mews house with a small countrified showroom containing fumed oak furniture and chintz, quite unlike the other major London dress houses. It was run on correspondingly meagre lines. The leading mannequin (or model) was already designing

Left: Lachasse Hardy Amies designs as drawn and sold to Altman's department store of New York. Blouses were and are an integral part of a woman's wardrobe, and were considered essential in the 1930s, to be worn under a suit jacket or simply with a skirt. Hardy Amies evolved many clever twists to his blouse designs, a perfect foil to his new ideas for suits. Note the Austrian source of the bottom image, an influence Hardy himself absorbed at this time, 1937.

S904

1939

for Mildred Shay

A Lachasse Hardy Amies suit design sketched by himself and showing the inspiration in the swatch of wool attached. The design of the skirt is now looser and moving towards the new bell shape. The detailing of the jacket exemplifies his way of adding spice to an otherwise staid design. The suit was designed in 1939 for a friend of Lady Jersey, the Hollwood screen actress Mildred Shay, who later wore his famous 'Made in England' suit to great acclaim (see pp.74–75).

A Lachasse Hardy Amies sketch for a late 1930s sophisticated suit. The detailing is clearly derived from Austro-German tracht popular with affluent skiers of the period and also related to the taste for Baroque and Rococo detailing in interior decoration and clothing. The upswept hair style reflects the Amies 'credo' of 1937, and his preference for long necks on models with similar hair styles.

the next collection, based on Morton's existing designs, but after her temperamental behaviour Hardy was asked by Shingleton if he felt capable of designing the August Collection.

Hardy always maintained that in joining Lachasse, he had 'come home'. This was not simply due to his mother's memories of her days with three court dressmakers, but because he had so often accompanied her to visit former colleagues, when he would be left in the care of the stockroom keeper, and could observe the work going on around him. Miss Gray Ltd. was certainly no trendsetter, but being close to Claridge's and the Mayfair houses of the affluent, it was patronised by women of taste wanting elegant well-made clothes which were in fashion, but not overpoweringly fashionable. It had five or six workrooms with one for embroidery. These observations, conversations with his mother and the knowledge he honed at Lachasse helped to form the backbone of his own post-war business at Savile Row, together with his instinctive taste and flair in designing for discerning women, most particularly in designing for Her Majesty Queen Elizabeth II.

The clientele at Lachasse (appropriately named for its original sporting form of clothes and clientele) mainly consisted of women seeking elegant country suits with a subtle twist to the cut and line, and a choice of superlative woollen fabrics. The suits had to be good enough to be worn on odd days in London, and eventually blend in with race meetings and other country pursuits, not ageing too rapidly in their style, as older suits were generally worn to less formal events. 'Morton's philosophy was to transform the suit from the strict tailleur, or the ordinary country tweed fit only for the moors, into an intricate and carefully-designed garment, so fashionable that it could be worn with confidence at the Ritz', as Hardy put it. (*SH* p.21)

Hardy talked to the international clientele, observed fittings, examined Digby Morton's remaining stock and dissected the component parts with the workforce, so that he thoroughly understood what the clients liked and why. The two head tailors, Mr Ernest and Mr Todd, together with the dressmaker Miss Joyce, collaborated with him to produce the new collection from his own designs, which also included day and evening dresses to complement the suits. His remaining sketches of the time display his ingenuity, and give the lie to his assertion that he could not sketch. Some have swatches attached, and in common with most designers he was often inspired by new textile samples revealing the latest designs and colours, brought to his door by a small army of sales representatives from an astonishing number of British companies, then producing many of the best textiles in the world.

Hardy's first collection in August 1934 was late in completion and also slow to move, but thanks to Shingleton's arrangement with the Harrogate dress business of Louis Copé, and Hardy's travelling salesman training, Amies took it up to Yorkshire and returned with a good order in advance of the London show. His future seemed secure: 'I rang up my mother in great glee' he recalled. Unknown to Hardy, she was already suffering from the early stages of terminal cancer, and would never experience his greatest success.

Lachasse Hardy Amies tour-de-force of detailing to a London suit on the eve of war in August 1939. Amies' ingenuity in detailing the back with gathered seams accentuates the waist, and a button-through skirt gives height. The relatively plain front allowed the owner's jewels and furs to provide any necessary decoration, as hinted at by the furred cuffs. Designed for Miss Adelaide Stanley, then appearing at the London Palladium and known for her appearance in an early BBC television transmission in 1938 of Beaumont's 1607 play The Knight of the Burning Pestle, *which would have appealed to Hardy Amies.*

Hardy later erroneously maintained that Lachasse had no rich or famous clients and was completely overlooked by the fashion press. In fact *Vogue*, *Harper's Bazaar* and very many other journals and newspapers, including the US magazine *Women's Wear Daily* (*WWD*) gave Lachasse a great deal of coverage, although the name of Hardy Amies only began to be mentioned from around January 1937, when *WWD* illustrated the 'sports clothes' (as Lachasse suits were still termed) ordered by Lady Mountbatten at Lachasse – it would have been difficult to be any more fashionable at that time.

The attraction of Hardy's inventive designs was augmented by their superlative fit. By 1936 his own taste and inherited genes manifested themselves strongly:

'The suits Morton had made in his last year with us had a comparatively short jacket, about 24.5" from the back of the collar to the waist, and they were high-waisted in the sense that they buttoned to just slightly above the natural waistline. One day I realised that if you lower the waistline to its lowest possible point, that is to say to the lowest point where it is also narrow, you have a much longer line from shoulder to waist, but what is more important, you have a longer line from under the arm-hole to the waist. This gives you much more room to move when in action, and makes the jacket lie almost peacefully on its own when you are still, the high-waisted effect having given you a buttoned up and restricted look. ...at this time the shoulders of the suits were also heavily padded. In order to counter-act the top-heavy look I lengthened the jackets, and over a season or two they became as long as 27.5". The total effect was to give a much more important-looking suit, and I was given greater scope, as I had more jacket to deal with to give emphasis to the hips, which was something quite unheard of for many years'. (*JSF* pp.61-62)

Hardy stressed that he did not wish to claim great originality as a designer, but the general proportions of his suits were copied from then on and throughout the war. Manufacturers of wholesale suits told him that they based their production on his designs. The press of the period noted Lachasse as appearing high on any list of visiting American buyers seeking suits in London before travelling on to Paris.

British couture became internationally important during the 1930s. London was still the centre of the Empire, attracting affluent visitors to an enormous number of attractions. Mayfair and Belgravia hummed with activity, regulated largely by the seasonal activities of the King and Queen, and reflected in the 'Court & Social' pages of newspapers and journals or seen in newsreels. The demand for couture clothes was such that in addition to the growing number of young British couture businesses, which soon competed with their established Parisian counterparts, some Parisian couture houses now opened branches in London, including Molyneux and Schiaparelli, adding to the established London Houses of Paquin and Worth.

The older and more conventional British Houses of Handley-Seymour and Reville-Terry supplied Queen Mary and other members of the Royal Family, but were rapidly being challenged by the seductive innovations of young

Hardy and Herbert flanking Mary Amies, already suffering from terminal cancer in 1935, photographed in the garden of Burleighs, Green Lane, Dagenham, Essex their last home on the Becontree Estate. Still standing and renamed 'The White House', the early nineteenth-century house is now bereft of its garden and surrounded by roads, but has found a new use as an Age Concern centre.

Norman Hartnell. For the last decade Hartnell had been burdened with the tag of 'Cambridge undergraduate designer' but in 1934 he moved into a large remodelled Bruton Street house across Berkeley Square with opulently *art-moderne* interiors, just as Lachasse was adjusting to life with Hardy Amies, who studied all and any competition with a keen eye. (*Be Dazzled!* pp.64-65)

Lachasse became a founder member of the Fashion Group of Great Britain, holding regular group shows for visiting buyers at glamorous hired locations, such as Claridges. Those with large Houses, such as Hartnell, gave coordinated shows in their own premises. Their chairwoman was Fashion Editor of *Vogue*. The George VI Coronation collections of 1937 brought even greater numbers of North Americans to London, and in April of that year Lachasse had its first full editorial page in British *Vogue* (known in its New York head office as 'Brogue') for the suit named 'Panic'. In the programme for the Fashion Group show of January 1938, the Lachasse page title had added (DESIGNER- HARDY AMIES). This attribution was the subject of one of many wrangles between Hardy and Shingleton, who feared losing his designer, as he had Morton.

Walking with style. Alexis and Anne ffrench accompany Hardy Amies on the coast around 1936. Anne's own Lachasse elegance is noticeable in the style of her coat, gauntled gloves, bag and hat. Weekends, holidays and weeks together in London, Kent, Essex or Cornwall were to be the comfortable pattern of their lives until Alexis died in 1956. Hardy wears a long cosy coat of teddy-bear fur, fashionable pre-war for casual wear and motoring.

lachasse

According to Amies, this logo dated from its inception of the company in 1928, before Digby Morton joined, although Morton has latterly been credited with the elegant design.

Fair and Square

Square shoulders and slimly cut—here is a smart coat with the herringbone used horizontally in Munroepun Authentic Scottish Tweed by

LACHASSE

Lachasse Hardy Amies: the luxury of soft, warm British tweed, handled with casual simplicity to form a wide-shouldered tweed overcoat with two slant pockets at the hips and small inset ones at the shoulder, the stand-up collar running into two pleats to the bottom of the arm-holes. A 1938 design forecasting the shape of the early 1940s.

In the late 1930s Hardy Amies designs became ever more inventive. The showcards up to 1939 include the usual fifty to sixty designs, all with appropriately pertinent and topical names, giving a flavour of the designer and his times. Spring 1935 included 'Spinney', 'Stirrup Cup', and 'Black Mischief '(Evelyn Waugh's novel just enjoyed). Amongst the Autumn 1937 designs were 'Brolly', 'London Fog', 'Chelsea Mist', 'Coq d'Or' (a favourite restaurant), 'Ritz Bar'(another favourite) and 'Oxford Accent'. In autumn 1938 'Hardy Annual' ended the collection.

1934 also brought Hardy a London replacement for his German mentor Jonny. Alexis ffrench was an urbane witty connoisseur and dealer in antique furniture, with a love of decoration. He had a daughter from a previous marriage and his wife Anne had two from hers. The ffrench family were respected for their kindness, taste and sense of style, all put at Hardy's disposal and fully reciprocated for the next five decades.

With them Hardy found the external family he had enjoyed in Germany, but this time a more worldly and sophisticated one. Anne ffrench was a customer of Digby Morton at Lachasse and was clearly impressed and amused by his replacement. For the next twenty-two years until Alexis' death, Hardy shared in their life. He began to spend weekends with Alexis in his remodelled country house, Leaders, near Wrotham in Kent. The ffrench way of life embraced separate town and country establishments for man and wife, and after a period of commuting to Mayfair from his parents house in Dagenham, Hardy was invited to share Alexis' flat in Pont Street, Belgravia, above the new Alexis ffrench shop. Hardy also became lifelong friends with Alexis' sister Yvonne, an historian and connoisseur-dealer in drawings, who lived round the corner from Lachasse in Hill Street with Countess Voss.

Other lasting friendships were established at this time, including the decorators Syrie Maugham and the young John Fowler, together with Fowler's friends the dealer Geoffrey Houghton-Brown, and Richard Timewell, later an influential director of Sotheby's. Around 1938, Hardy also developed a friendship with his client Lady Jersey, who had been briefly married to Cary Grant, and (as Virginia Cherrill) had starred in Charlie Chaplin's 1931 film *City Lights*.

Nina Leclercq was to become a vital part of Hardy's own post-war business. A cousin of Michel de Brunhoff (editor of French *Vogue*), and of Lucien Vogel, (owner of 'Le Jardin des Modes'), both men were close to publisher Condé Nast himself, and Nina was unsurprisingly appointed as Assistant Fashion Editor of London *Vogue*. She and the artist Francis Marshall went with Hardy to observe the fashions at Cheltenham Races, but it poured with rain and they only observed macs; it became an event that cemented their friendship.

With his friends Hardy discussed the arts, especially literature, opera and fashion, and collected a large library of books on the history of costume. He was befriended by the designers Charles James, a fanatical experimenter with dress construction, and Victor Stiebel. Edward Molyneux, who sometimes visited his London branch, most inspired Hardy with his rigorous elimination of extraneous detail, sometimes even too much for Hardy, but an ultimate ideal and challenge to his own designs. (JSF, SH)

Lachasse Hardy Amies glamorous and elegant dresses from late 1939.

Below: A special design for a client with an off-the shoulder soft romantic dress with ruched neckline above a fitted bodice echoed in the banding swirling around the skirt just below the knees.

Right: A highly sophisticated fitted double-breasted short striped jacket over a slim fitted skirt, for the Countess of Jersey and worn with a turban.

Bottom right: A long flared double-breasted plain evening coat with military collar possibly also for the Countess of Jersey. The other names on the designs refer to those designated by Hardy to execute the work.

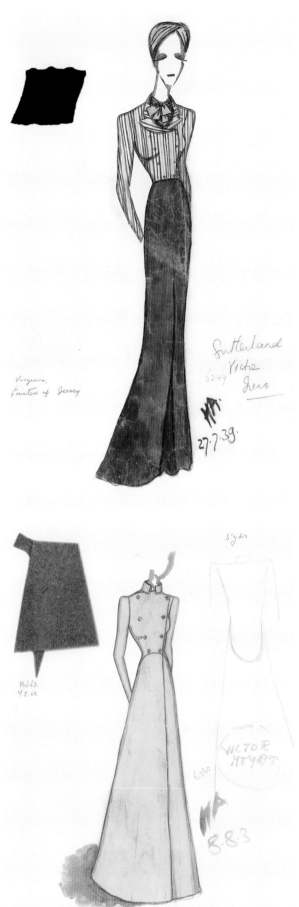

A scooped neckline of the Edwardian inspired taffeta dress with a tight bodice and leg o'mutton sleeves above the narrow striped skirt gathered at the back to a faux double bustle fullness. The dress was modelled in the June 1939 issue of Vogue by the actress June Duprez who had recently shot to fame in the film 'The Four Feathers'. 'Her Lachasse dress is news too' said Vogue. (Photo John Rawlings/Vogue © The Condé Nast Publications Ltd.)

6300

Lachasse Hardy Amies ultra-sophisticated evening dress with wide-shouldered jacket . A symphony of stripes, both horizontal and chevron, with Amies' trademark showstopping attention to the rear, here concentrated on a boldly-gathered trailing panel which appears below a softly-draped framing ruffle. Joyce and Irene were his two most trusted hands for such skilled work.

Learning at Lachasse

The world-renowned designer of tweeds and Sports Suits for Lachasse suggests these courts of unusual design to wear with this ensemble

★Lotus 8004, as illustrated, a smartly original court in brown glacé kid. Also available in black glacé kid, at 23/9.

LOTUS & DELTA
SHOES FOR WOMEN
OBTAINABLE AT GOOD SHOE SHOPS IN ALL THE LARGER TOWNS

A 1937 advertisement showing the type of shoes suitable to be worn with an Amies ensemble featuring his 'Bulkie', the sporty full jacket over a finely detailed suit with gored skirt. Lotus & Delta were sure of their choice and their text underlines Hardy's growing success and fame as a 'world-renowned designer'.

In 1937 Hardy introduced 'The Bulkie', a wide-shouldered loosely-fitted straight jacket, falling to just below the hips, and made from thick wool with wider revers. It was a feminine version of a type of stevedores' jacket with elements of American footballers' padded outlines, seen in many of the American films Hardy enjoyed, in which the costume designer Adrian's sleek fashions featured a similar silhouette. Youthful, practical and warm, it was a perfect jacket for women now adept at driving, and wanting to slip in and out of their cars without the volume of restricting coat skirts. The New York store Henri Bendel featured a Lachasse 'Bulkie' in their advertising as the 'straight-and-square' silhouette.

In July 1937 the audiences for his July collections took home a printed design forecast, typically Amies:

```
                        C R E D O

WE BELIEVE IN:

          A MORE FLUID SILHOUETTE
          Wide, softly padded shoulders.
          Small waists.

          CIRCULAR SKIRTS
          No more seated skirts.
          (Learn how to walk and swing a graceful hem.
          Be young and yet have poise).
          16 ins. off the ground.

          STRAIGHT SKIRTS STILL FOR THE TIMID
          and for the very short.
          Cunning pleats.
          Length 14½ - 15 ins. off the ground.

          JACKETS OF SUITS THAT ARE SNUG ON THE HIPS
          and as long as a circular skirt will permit.

          TOP JACKETS OVER SUITS
          Waisted, seamed and shaped over hips.
          One button to fasten or double breasted.

          CIRCULAR BASQUES ON TOWN SUITS
          Bone straight skirts.
          Fur.

          ACCENT ON LA BELLE POITRINE

          STREET SUITS
          A thick woollen dress with whirling skirt and tiny jacket.

          HUSKY TOP COATS
          in firm checked camel-hairs and plaids.

          PIDGEON-BLOOD RED
          All reds, from crimson lake to coral.

          UPBRUSHED HAIR
          No curls to be worried by
          COSY UPSTANDING COLLARS WITH OR WITHOUT FUR

          TINY HATS


                    -----oOo-----


          THE MAKE-UP AND HAIRDRESSING are by Elizabeth Arden Ltd.
          and we are grateful for their co-operation.
```

42

Lachasse Hardy Amies. The Coronation Collection of 1937 included this suit named 'Panic', for a reason Amies could not remember, except that it amused him. The tweed of dark plum with specks of vivid cerise criss-crossed with a large overcheck in emerald green was spotted as a reject in a Cumberland tweed mill glowing in a corner. It was made into this suit, which brought him his first whole editorial page in British Vogue, 14 April, 1937. His own name was still not mentioned. (Photo Cecil Beaton/Vogue © The Condé Nast Publications Ltd.)

Lachasse Hardy Amies, a finely-pleated short evening dress with plain mid-riff gathered at the back with a draped bow, the wartime refinements of design possible even with restrictive rationing, but still in the mood of the 1939 yellow dress design opposite.

1938 was a disturbing year, not least for Hardy Amies. Hitler threatened war and Austria voted to become part of the Third Reich, whilst unease spread throughout Europe as Czechoslovakia was threatened. Largely isolationist, America remained expansive in mood as their recession lessened. Amies designs of the period echo the earlier Parisian flirtation with Central European traditional peasant *tracht*, seen in the bell-like shape of skirts, puffed sleeves and gathered yokes of blouses and dresses. Hardy's jacket and skirt designs include references to the German country clothes he knew and saw once again, when he accompanied his father and sister to Austria and Germany on holiday following the death of his mother Mary in August 1938. Rosemary had returned from Berlin to be with her mother at the end, having tried to work in London at Jacqmar and then in Alexis ffrench's shop.

Right: *Lachasse Hardy Amies for summer 1939, the chic pared-down details of the soft pleats gathered at the waist and the shoulders with puff-sleeves forming a fashionable style almost set for the duration of the war.*

Below: *Lachasse Hardy Amies on the eve of war with a white bell-shaped dress edged with the same patterned cloth of the jacket with contrasting white revers, the blouse with string cross-lacing and a neat matching hat, perfect for Cannes.*

Father and daughter finished their holiday in a blacked-out Munich and rushed back to London, where Rosemary stayed with her father until he re-married in 1939. Hardy paid a last visit to Bendorf, where he had passionate discussions with Jonny about the international situation.

Another person resident in Austria at that time was Alexis ffrench's's eldest brother Conrad O'Brien-ffrench, who had been based since 1935 in Kitzbuhl, as Agent Z3 of the Secret Service. He had warned London in March 1938 of German troops massing near the border, before his cover was blown, and he was to prove significant in Hardy's future.

Lachasse clothes were now regularly bought and advertised by discerning American stores such as Henri Bendel in New York, with the Amies name given due credit in the press. Hardy had become adept at creating suits using a variety of woollen cloths and by cleverly using self-striped ones to form unusual geometric patterns. His detailing of the backs of garments became (and remained) famous, as did unusual and striking colour combinations. Ideas for blouses to be worn under suit jackets were sold to Altman's, then a great New York store; cloth and shoe makers were amongst those giving free publicity in their advertising to Lachasse, but not specifically to Hardy, whose natural ambition was thwarted, as he saw it, by the heavy hand of Shingleton.

Conversations with his friends and his own observations had set his ideas on design. 'Less is more' was his life-long belief, and his last season before war in September 1939 was a summing-up of his achievements so far in his thirtieth year. In these last peacetime designs, Hardy seems to sum up life with the ffrench family, the enjoyment of escorting their daughters to dances and restaurants, the press noting his increasingly youthful clientele, which ordered more evening wear and even wedding dresses with trousseaus including: 'Most enchanting town suits .. racing people come here too... [from] Newmarket, Cheltenham and Liverpool... Mr Hardy gives two fittings and a finished fitting, or just two for a plain tweed suit from about 13 guineas. Evening dresses cost from 13 guineas up... cut with wonderful slick perfection.' (*Eve's Journal*, January 1939)

The 1939 spring collection of ninety-four models was the largest ever. Fashion editor Alison Settle noted the tight bodices and full skirts, whilst the Hardy Amies dress card explained how the new shape was created: 'The corsets are executed by our own corsetiere.' This was the basis for both Amies' new barrel shape for jackets, and his romantic dresses worn at Court by several women. The best examples were illustrated in *Harpers*,

Lachasse Hardy Amies, the designer exemplifying his own elegant approach to male dress on holiday in Cannes with Alexis ffrench and Nina Leclercq, late Spring 1939.

and featured Alençon lace over parma violet taffeta, a reference to Empress Eugenie. *Vogue* summed up the collection by commenting that English designers had never before been so free of the influence of Paris and its rush for novelties and were thinking in terms of their individual clientele. (*Vogue*, March 1939)

Hardy, Alexis and Nina Leclercq left for Cannes, a last glorious late spring holiday of peace and elegant living, as the face of oncoming war became apparent. Hardy reflected on what had happened to him since he last stood as a penniless schoolboy in Antibes - now he boldly marched into the casino.

By July Alison Settle reported in *The Star* that US buyers 'had again come to London before the Paris Collections' and were buying. *Harpers* USA contained a Macy's full page advertisement of a copy of a Lachasse bought original.

Hardy wrangled with Shingleton, then signed a new three year contract. The Lachasse order books filled steadily and their workrooms hummed; outside war drums were beating.

Lachasse Hardy Amies, the famous Vogue March 1939 image of the reintroduction of the boned corset into London fashion, predates the famous image by Horst in 1940. Most women wore foundation garments of some type to achieve the smooth lines necessitated by the close-fitted dresses or suits of the period, Hardy Amies was making a good publicity point in dramatising the changing pre-war silhouette emphasising tiny waists and fuller bosoms, the basis of post-war fashion. (Photo Arik Nepo/Vogue © The Condé Nast Publications Ltd.)

FOR KING AND COUNTRY

Hardy Amies

For King and Country

Previous page: *Echoes of war. The remains of Hardy Amies'uniforms indicating his rank, designation to the Intelligence Corps and parachute training. This would have been worn on the left sleeve of the uniform jacket.*

Below: *The Intelligence Corps badge as embellished later by Hardy Amies. He claimed that someone had jokingly told him it represented 'a pansy resting on its laurels'.*

Right: *Hardy Amies (centre) the new recruit at war, and bottom in full uniform. 1940.*

On 1 September 1939 Germany invaded Poland, and two days later Britain and France declared war on Germany. Hardy wrote, 'once the shock of the calamity of war had worn off, I began to accept it philosophically. To me, as I think to many others, it was to be an escape'. (*JSF* p.72)

He had come to an impasse with his career at Lachasse. Frustration with the lack of public acknowledgement of his name, as the talent responsible for the growing success of the company and the intransigence of the owner, Mr Shingleton, who ensured that he was referred to merely as 'Mr Hardy' and, apart from a birthday gift of Lachasse shares, was not overly generous. His wife 'Miss Gray' had died in 1937 so Hardy no longer had his mediator, and he believed that Shingleton protected his investment in a selfish manner. Shingleton was interviewed in October 1939 '...his ruddy good health more like a farmer than a dressmaker. "But I am that too... I breed shorthorn cattle...We are ploughing up a thousand acres for the duration... with six tractors." ' (*Observer*, 15 October 1939) He had turned down Hardy's suggestion that they move to the larger defunct Miss Gray premises in Brook Street and re-open a large House under Hardy's name. Every move, any change, had become a battle between him, the supervisory management at   Paulette and its owner, worried that Hardy might leave, as Digby Morton had done.

The last echo of peace came with this 1938 collection described by Alison Settle: 'The colour of autumn leaves arrived in his gingerbread tweeds and spice cloth trimmed with golden fox. Moving though it was, the show finished with the entry of mannequins in procession, wearing fine wool dinner dresses, each carrying a silver candelabra.' 'That is symbolic of carrying the candle of British trade.' Hardy told her. (*Observer*, 19 October, 1938)

In the same month *Vogue* profiled Hardy as 'thin, energetic and shrewd... the managing designer of Lachasse. He is a very live wire indeed, with smart ideas on decor as well as designing. This young man has developed his talent with remarkable speed.' It described the now chintzless interiors with stone and parquet floors and cyclamen washed walls, 'There are rope banisters up the staircase...the armchairs are covered in mouse-brown linen, softly piped with blue ...a charming interior, not unlike a very smart kitchen.' (*Vogue*, October, 1938)

Hardy had stamped his mark on the collections, the interiors and created a complete, sleek Lachasse look. He wanted more reward.

Hardy Amies in business under his own name. Part of the government-sponsored export drive aimed at raising currency abroad, and as propaganda by boosting the image of Britain abroad, in this instance in neutral Turkey, also targeted by similar German schemes. The multicoloured coordinated coat and suit, worn over a slate blue blouse, features a skirt with contrasting panels front and back and further promotes British manufacturers. Autumn 1943.

KA.
6.6.39.

War proved to be the catalyst. The Lachasse building was requisitioned as the local fire station, and Hardy duly joined the fire brigade, although he longed for a more productive role. Later in life he recalled seeing a mysterious advertisement in the personal column of *The Times* for the Corps of Military Police seeking those with a knowledge of at least two European languages. 'I wrote in at once' he stressed. Soon he was at Aldershot, becoming Private Amies No 7686146 in what was the beginning of the Field Security Police, which later became the Intelligence Corps. Always reticent about the exact details of his wartime activities, his own skeletal accounts have now been augmented by recent research into the few remaining papers of the period.

In mid-December 1939 he was returned home to await further instructions pending transfer to an Officers Training Unit. Shingleton was relieved to have him back designing the spring 1940 Lachasse collection, and never one to lose a photo opportunity, Hardy appeared in his uniform for the press. For this last collection at Lachasse made before the full restrictions of rationing hit, his fashion statement read:

'An easy silhouette. Padded, but not unnatural shoulders to accentuate a narrow waist. Skirts fullish, 16.5"-17" off the ground. All exaggeration disappearing in soft unpressed pleats. Some straight skirts, particularly with the return of the comfortable boxjacket. Many dresses with jackets, especially JERKINS, with the JERKIN NECKLINE. Soothing pastels and HOME BROWNS.'

Brown always remained a favourite Amies colour. To many it is not the most alluring of shades, but it is significant that all sources on the meaning of colour identify the personality of the brown-lover as one liking wholesome and earthy things, having a steadfast character imbued with a friendly and dependable disposition in a healthy body. All true of Hardy Amies.

The end of his training coincided with the debacle of Dunkirk, for which he might have been needed, followed by six weeks training for the Intelligence Corps. In the autumn of 1940 he was posted to the Canadian Corps headquarters near Leatherhead, where the Senior Intelligence Officer was John 2nd Baron Tweedsmuir (son of novelist John Buchan who had been Governor General of Canada from 1935-40), who sent for him just before Christmas with the words 'Your country needs you at last. You are to help open up another front for us: in South America'. (*JSF* p.77) Hardy was to participate in a Board of Trade promotion and propaganda scheme to send a combined collection of couture clothes. 'You can be spared', was the laconic comment from Tweedsmuir.

The collection was to be shown in Buenos Aires, Rio de Janeiro, Montevideo and Sao Paulo in April 1941 and reveals how far up the fashion tree Amies had climbed. In the order advertised, Molyneux, Norman Hartnell, Creed, Lachasse, Digby Morton, Paquin, Peter Russell, Victor Stiebel and Worth were the designers selected to show, and it proved to be a great success. The work in designing for this collection in

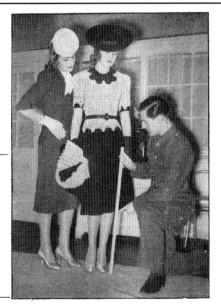

Opposite page: *A Hardy Amies headline-making innovation from the Lachasse 1939 Spring Collection, freaturing the barrel shape for his jackets. A short-lived fashion which generated many orders, it was killed off by the outbreak of war in September 1939.*

Above: *A Hardy Amies at Lachasse design for a 1939 suit with a plain skirt and striped barrel jacket, a luxurious contrast to the incoming simplified styles seen below.*

Right: *Soon after the outbreak of war Hardy Amies joined the army. His established reputation as a designer was such that he was given permission to continue designing during his free time, at the request of the Board of Trade in order to participate in various export and domestic schemes related to the design and production of women's clothing. The change of silhouette, seen here inside Lachasse, is noticeable.*

Now a private in the Army, Mr. Hardy Amies, Lachasse dress designer, wearing ordinary "Tommy's" uniform, spent his last day of leave last week completing 1940 spring designs. Photo shows him at work with mannequins at the showrooms.

Hardy Amies (centre in helmet) after qualifying as a parachutist at RAF Ringway, 1942. Although he knew that he would never be sent abroad on a mission, he felt that he had to go through and appreciate the same rigorous training as those who went, in order to gain some insight into what they would experience.

part led to the final row over terms and conditions with Shingleton, who told Hardy he was too big for his boots ('It was true') and ignoring Hardy's financial problems – he was now living on his savings, had no army pay and nothing from Lachasse. He was fired.

On 2 January 1941 he noted in his diary that he had lunch at the Ritz with the celebrated bohemian socialite Viva King – and so his wartime pattern of life readjusted itself to off-duty lunches and dinners with friends, such as John Fowler with whom he sometimes stayed at Odiham, fellow designers Edward Molyneux and Digby Morton, and weekends or breaks with Alexis ffrench in London or the cottage in Kent. The singer Olga Lynn and her friend Maud Nelson became regular dining companions. Rosemary was now with the National Fire Service Service and Hardy saw his father, stepmother and brother Wilfred from time to time. He had become a proficient tennis player whilst in Birmingham and played during the summer months.

Now began one of the strangest of many unusual wartime careers, as Hardy balanced his military training with a necessarily part-time career as a designer in off-duty moments. He lacked a fashion house of his own, but was a respected and established name in fashion circles, and most importantly he was in the orbit of American buyers. Alys Ziegler of New York store Henri Bendel gave him the first of his independent orders, and Viyella requested dresses to feature in their advertising. But all of this was of little use if he failed to find the necessary hands to produce the clothes.

In Coronation year 1937 he had shared a taxi with the Fashion Editor of *Vogue*, Madge Garland, who encouraged him: 'Mark my words Hardy, you are on the road to going far'. Madge was by now Director of Fashion at Bourne & Hollingsworth on Oxford Street, one of the many great stores of the period. To his great relief, Hardy was given facilities in their workroom, and he celebrated by sitting in the Hyde Park Hotel writing his signature on a wide white satin ribbon to be embroidered as his label, still in use today.

Feet firmly on the wool: Second Lieutenant Amies designing his early wartime collection.

in
MUNROSPUN
AUTHENTIC
TWEED

Further Outlook Unsettled

A disturbance centred around this cyclone skirt is spreading rapidly over Europe and America. Worn under a trim jacket in Munrospun Authentic Scottish Tweed. The hat is by Aage Thaarup

THE SUIT BY LA CHASSE

'Further Outlook Unsettled', the new Amies-Lachasse bell-shaped skirt with a dirndl twist to the cut featuring the horizontal join to the boldly-checked tweed. Plaids and checks became highly fashionable amongst the leading Parisian couturiers following the State Visit to France in 1938, and were used in deference to the Scottish ancestry of Queen Elizabeth, consort of King George VI, who caused a sensation in her all-white Hartnell designs. As the caption notes 'A disturbance centred around this cyclone skirt is spreading over Europe and America'. The hat was by Aage Thaarup (1906-87), a favourite milliner to Queen Elizabeth, the two Princesses and Princess Marina, Duchess of Kent and many stars throughout the 1940s and 1950s. Amies used Thaarup hats in several of his post-war collections. This brought his designs of dirndl-inspired bell-shaped skirts to a close until his own post-war evolution of the idea was apparent in his coat designs echoing the New Look (page 85).

Good in any material!

size 36.

Button spacing as on black suit, and same on overcoat

bigger bust

HA
18·5·40

*Todd
Sutherland
Moya*

*Stock
64488 2*

As time went on he found a new home, shared with other designers in the Worth House at 50 Grosvenor Street. His interests were looked after by Miss Campbell, 'Cammie', formerly of Lachasse, and in 1942 he was one of the founder members of The Incorporated Society of London Fashion Designers (INCSOC) which superseded The London Fashion Group, and who were concerned with presenting a united front of designers dealing with promotion at home and overseas, as well as the manufacture of elegant and practical Utility clothing for women coping with the rationing system.

By 1942, out of some 30,000 clothing factories, only about 1,500 had not been turned over to other war work, Most of the workforce had been drafted to munitions factories, so attractive and varied clothing

Above left: The Earl and Countess of Jersey at home. Lady Jersey, the former film star Virginia Cherrill, was a good client and friend to Hardy Amies, here serving as a fine advertisement for his latest suit designs, photographed at Osterley Park, spring 1940. The suit (above and below left) was no 15 'Salmon and Cucumber' in the spring 1940 Collection. Made of heavy pastel-toned Cumberland tweed, the fitted jacket had squared shoulders and a bias-cut skirt with four unpressed pleats.

Above: *Hardy Amies; the practical shape for a British woman's suit during wartime. Minimum detailing and use of cloth, sensible shoes and large bag for travelling and emergencies. 1941*

Right: *A Hardy Amies design for a suit of the same period. Nipped in waists and minimal pleats to the skirt. 1941*

designs were vital. Hardy and Molyneux found the lack of applied decorative detail, minimum number of seams, buttons, pleats and other rules just a reflection of their own design skills, and the use of man-made fibres, such as rayon, or greater use of cotton an interesting challenge. In 1940 it was reported that: 'Yorkshire woollen manufacturers are experimenting with fibres from inside peanut shells, the fluffy extract mixed with wool.' (*News Review*, 1 August, 1940)

By 1943 American rationing also affected his designs and *WWD* illustrated his latest dresses and suits with curved hips and straight silhouettes softened at neck and waist by soft bows and the skirts with gathered panels to the front and back, also seen in the sparse pages of the British fashion press. Hardy stated boldly: 'Austerity presents no problems to me. Actually, I like it because it shows up a designer's ability and the skill of his work-rooms as more elaborate styles rarely do.' Such

Left: *A Hardy Amies summer suit, the light fabric jacket with military-inspired patch pockets, and skirt with the prescribed faux box pleats. 1943*

Below: *In 1940 Hardy Amies set up his own business within the Worth House at 50 Grosvenor Street. Also sharing the premises was Victor Stiebel, also serving in the armed forces.*

was the increasing scarcity of clothes in the shops, that *Vogue* tried to encourage its readers to remember '...these things remain ...colour, cut, fabric, accessories, grooming', a concept allied to government schemes such as 'Make Do and Mend'.

The counterpart of Hardy's life lay in his work for the Intelligence Service, first training at Beaulieu, where he formed lasting friendships with fellow trainees such as the author and screenwriter Paul Dehn, who, like James Bond author Ian Fleming, had been sent to Camp-X in Canada, classicist and later politician Enoch Powell, and author Patrick Leigh-Fermor. His eventual transfer on recommendation, almost certainly with the backing of Alexis ffrench's brother Conrad, was to the offices of T–Section in Baker Street, dealing with activity in Belgium. T–Section were part of the Special Operations Executive (SOE) formed to 'coordinate all action by way of sabotage and subversion against the enemy overseas'. He began on November 24 1941.

For King and Country

Hardy Amies rings the wartime fashion changes with innovative choices from the decreasing selection of fabrics, and strictly adhering to the government guidelines covering every detail from the number of buttons to the types of seams and decorative details. 1943

Opposite page: *Hardy Amies design for The Cotton Board's 'Colour, Design and Style' centre in Manchester, set up to promote the possibilities of British cotton in high fashion. In spring 1942 he designed three models with large dolman sleeves and a dropped waistline, a new silhouette. This dress was in a brown and cream print by Joseph Bridge of Manchester, and the designs were created with export firmly in mind. (© Victoria and Albert Museum, London)*

Apart from his assessment reports, now in the National Archives, and his own brief outline of events, his sparse entries in his desk and pocket diaries give his movements and some indication of particular missions (often named after Shakespearean characters) involving T–Section agents with a variety of ingenious names to stand out in wireless transmissions. (National Archives) Nothing else seems to remain. Nor are there any diaries or papers dating from before 1940.

From September 1943 his number two was a young schoolmaster, Colin Tivey, also sent on the recommendation of a senior colleague: 'he really understands the continental mind'. The third leading officer was naturalist Gavin Maxwell, who specialised in fieldcraft and had trained in Scotland. Maxwell suffered from a duodenal ulcer and was reported in January 1944 as having 'an excitable temperament and egotistical to a degree', possibly his ill health having a bad effect. Hardy told Colin Tivey, 'After the war you will teach at Winchester and I shall dress the Duchess of Westminster.' (Author conversation with Mrs Colin Tivey) The latter did indeed come true.

Of the war, Hardy wrote, 'To be honest, any latent patriotism or burning desire to defend the Homeland was only fully aroused at the Battle of Britain. At no time could I bring myself to a fighting hatred of the Germans. How often was I to hear 'the only good Hun is dead Hun', and how often was I to notice that it was not the most lively of Englishmen who intoned these words.'(*JSF* p.72)

Early section reports of Hardy's progress were largely positive: 'Although not military by disposition ..he is improving with experience.' Major-General Sir Colin McVean Gubbins KCMG, DSO, MC was the main force in SOE, and appended, 'I concur. He is intelligent and quick.' Privately, Hardy later blamed Gubbins for the debacle over a Lee Miller *Vogue* feature from liberated Brussels, which left him without the British military decoration he might have expected for his work. Even before this, his superior officer Brigadier Mockler-Ferryman had assessed Hardy's performance, 'Pleasant personality and an intelligent young officer. A good French and German linguist who takes considerable interest in his work, who mixes well with his Belgian opposite numbers and contacts generally. Sometimes gives the impression of immaturity, but on the whole his judgement can be relied on. No opportunity of appreciating his military qualities, but his command over his officers and other ranks is satisfactory.' Gubbins begrudging comment was: 'Concur. A little bit colourless, but does his work satisfactorily.' This was certainly not the opinion of those who worked with him, and he later wrote, 'In dealing with the more secret departments of the British War Office, I realised that there was no more, intriguing, cunning and touchy person than a high-ranking officer in such departments. But the tiresome thing about the whole boring procedure was that I was not allowed to talk about anything, and I rather like talking.'(*JSF* p.109)

Hardy mastered all the difficult tasks set him, including liaising with the representatives of the Deuxieme Bureau and the Sûreté Department of the Belgian Government-in-Exile, themselves unwilling to allow a full-scale

coat 1½ check
1 yd Plain
cape. 1½ yd Plain

Victor
Alice
Bligh.
5894

Hardy Amies designs for two examples of elegant simplicity from late 1939, before rationing made embroidery and frivolous capes impossible. The concept of these designs illustrates why Amies had no difficulty in designing to rigid guidelines, and why he enjoyed the challenge.

Overleaf: A letter to his sister and sketches from Brussels in September 1944. The designs were for his London workrooms, the last sketch of the 'Zazou' (on page 73) depicts a style adopted as a gesture of defiance against the German occupiers, and copies the long jacket similarly invented by the youth of Montparnasse. Hardy Amies wrote 'It was flamboyant, sexy in an abandoned sort of way, and horribly inelegant, but it was provocative ... to make it graceful it had to turn into the New Look.' (JSF p.106)

operation against collaborators and traitors in Belgium in January 1944, and anxious about German reprisals against a population already suffering great hardship. The Belgian operation, now known as 'Rat Week' was intended to end the terrible losses of agents sent from London and those on the ground, who not only committed acts of sabotage, but also ran the Cométe Line aiding Allied forces to escape, mainly through France to Spain. The most corrupt offender targeted by Hardy, Prosper Dezitter, evaded capture until after the end of the war. However T–Section was far from being a failure, agents did get through with cash, and supplies were dropped successfully. After D-Day, when the Allied Forces seemed on the verge of being unable to capture a deep-water harbour vital for the routing of supplies, the only remaining port was that of Antwerp, which was snatched from under the noses of the arriving German reinforcements, largely due to the prompt actions of those linked to T–Section. In September 1944 Hardy was sent to liberated Brussels.

Todd
Alice

Myra
for Meredith
5844

Blue Flannel

Spring 1943
Number Twelve

Suit in navy cloth - white pique shirt.

Stock 103
Leonard Matthews

Spring 1943
Beige - soft, thick hard overcoat
or Camelhair & grosgrain lapella & patch flaps.

Number eleven

Stock No: 103
Leonard & ditto

Log belt at back & vent

The Hardy Amies designs above for a late 1939 coat and suit are in stark contrast to those left, created in 1942 and 1943. The construction of the later coat and jacket displays the straightforward form of the wide padded shoulders, compared to the work involved in the puffed leg o'mutton–like sleeves of those seen above left and right, when materials and labour were easily available.

Dear Peg,

For a long while I have wanted to write to you but we
have had little spare time and also I am having such trouble with
my fountain pen, that I have put it off until my charming and
faithful secretary has a moment to do this letter for me. We are
such old friends that you can excuse the impersonal note and merely
profit from the legibility.

Although it was planned that I should leave London for
Brussels very early in September, a series of circumstances in
London prevented this and I did not get out here until about a
fortnight after Brussels had been liberated. Some of the officers
of our department were, however, among the first to enter this city
and they very shrewdly secured comfortable quarters for us, of which
more anon.

I actually left England on Wednesday, 20th September,
but returned to London for a few days after that and finally came
to Brussels a week later on the 27th. The two journeys out I made
in a small bomber put at the disposal of this Mission. The lack of
comfort in the plane was made up by the increase in weight allowed
us so that we were able to bring out considerable quantities of food-
stuffs, which we had been warned, quite rightly, would be scarce in
Brussels. The journey was uneventful except for the excellent views
of the flying bomb sites on the French coast and the feeling of
exhileration at leaving England for the first time in five and a
half years.

Although the first frenzy of excitement had died down,
there was still considerable disorder in Brussels, even at that time.
In the background was the lack of stability due to the disolution
of the Government. The unhappy situation regarding the prisoner
King was quickly bettered by the installation of the Regent on
Thursday, 21st September, I was lucky enough to get a ticket for the
ceremony which I shall never forget. The enthusiastic reception of
the Regent was only equalled by that given to the Queen Mother and to
Cardinal van Roey. The large and picturesque hats of the ladies of
the diplomatic corps fitted well into the Louis Philippe classicism of
the Senate Chamber.

Our offices are in an old building on the boulevard
which crosses the Quartier Leopold. It was formerly the headquarters
of part of the Luftwaffe, who conveniently left behind some excellent
maps on the walls and comfortable, if rather flashy furniture. We
also procured the officers living quarters which are in flats in a
modern building almost a stone's throw away. These flats are
hidiously, but conveniently furnished. By some miracle there was a
large stock of coke for the furnaces so that we have had central
heating and hot water until now, when we have managed to get our
Army rations. I have a small flat to myself on the 7th floor with
a wonderful view over the roofs of the old hotels of the Quartier
Leopold. Our Mess is in a large flat on the 4th floor of the same
building. The Germans, either in haste, or as I trust from decency,
left behind even easily transportable bibelots. We have procured the
services of an excellent Belgian couple as cook and Mess waiter and

Black &
White
check

Centre
seam
to back of
skirt

Jacket overcoat
161

161

we are able to prove daily that British Army rations are excellent
if properly cooked. We have managed to obtain enough drink for
our modest requirements from stocks the Germans left behind, or
which were hidden from them by the tenacious Belgians. As far as
the physical man is concerned, war is not too bad a hell.

The wonderful reception given to the fighting troops has not
cooled as regards staff officers like ourselves. The hospitality
offered us has been overwhelming. In the early days this hospitality took the form of enormous and fantastic meals offered to us
at restaurants at still more enormous and fantastic prices. These
restuarants were, of coursem kept open deliberately by the Germans
to encourage the black market and the Belgian chefs revelled in
the opportunity of displaying their art without restriction. You
could literally have anything you wanted. One had, however, a slightly
guilty feeling and no-one regrets the recent laws closing all the
restuarants. It is, of course, the intention to re-open them with
fixed prices as in England as soon as normal stocks at normal prices
can be obtained. This will take a little time and the first task of
the Government, aided as they are now by the Army, is to see that
the housewife is able to get her ration coupons honoured; this is
just beginning to take place.

The black market, however, still continues in a modified form.
Do not judge this harshly and remeber, firstly that throughout the
four years of occupation, it has been the Belgians duty to evade all
forms of restriction in order not to help the Germans, and secondly
that all the machinery for the control and distribution of food was
in the hands of German created organisation which were immediately
cancelled by Belgian Government decree after the liberation, and
alas, before the new organisations were ready and able to function
efficiently. Not as small factor has been the breakdown in the
monetary system. Part of the German's demoralisation policy was
to flood Belgium with Belgian paper money. The Government has att-
empted to stop inflation by blocking old notes and issuing fresh.
If this has had the desired result in wiping out fortunes acquired
during the war, it also restricts present trade and production.
Production is also held up owing to the lack of machinery and basic
materials, so that commodities remain extremely scarce and prices
are still fantasically high. It has been said, quite rightly,
that Belgium is now a country where you can find all the super-
fluous luxuries of life, but none of the necessities. You can find
bottles of pre-war Ouerlin without difficulty, but there is no pepper.

This letter is getting altogether into too serious a vein to
go further into economics, but I cannot help feeling overwhelmed
by the tremendous problems which await us after this war. The whole
of the economic structure of the country has been destroyed, firstly
by the Germans and secondly by the Belgians of their own free will,
acting under the orders of the Allied Commanders. The cry during the
occupation was sabotage and it has now turned to reconstruction.
This complete volte-face cannot be achieved in two months.

Let us now turn to brighter things. I have already spoken
of the early hospitality offered to us in restaurants. We are still
offered magnigicient meals in private houses, particularly in the
country, where there is often plenty of eggs, butter and fowl.
Often almost a glut, owing to the difficulties of transporting
these articles to the towns. But we also do not overlook the fact
that Belgian hostesses will use up all their available rations and
stocks carefully hidden from the Germans to give us stupendous meals
in the true Belgian tradition. It was a wonderful and pleasant
shock to see again the ceremony of a continental dinner with the
unceasing changing of plates by white-gloved servants, who, excellent
and born waiters as they are, never leave even one of the many
glasses at your side unfilled. The basis of a Belgian dinner is,
of course, the Burgundy, and the man proud of his cellar will give
you two or three kinds. I remember one Sunday luncheon for twenty-
four people which started at one o'clock with old Port and ended
at five o'clock in the afternoon with home-made Cassis. This host

"Blueberry"
plain back to
shirt with
buttons:

plain back to skirt

157

Dorelia

had hidden his wines in various parts of his estate and each bottle
seemed, not only to have a history, but a war anecdote. Parties are,
however, getting less gargantuan and as hostesses know us better,
they ask us to send, for instance, some margarine and lard round
on the morning of the dinner as fats are so scarce and are needed
in the sources which are the pride of the Belgian cooks. Particu-
ularly delicious, and which I do not remember having in France, are
the green soups made of cress, watercress and often chervil which is
grown in quantities.

I must, however, insist that these feasts are all occasions;
there is very little meat in the shops and in family circles
vegeterian dishes are the rule. They are, however, so deliciously
cooked that it is no hardship to be invited to them.

One of the most interesting jobs of the officers of this Mission
has been to visit the headquarters of the various resistance groups
throughout the country. Without doing this, it is impossible to
imagine how deeply resistance has penetrated into the roots of the
community. Everyone, from the aristocrats and bankers to the poorest
peasants worked in his orn particular way against the Germans. The
former by distrubuting funds clandestinely to families whose bread-
earners had either been deported to Germany or hidden in the maquis.
The latter by arranging grounds where arms and men were parachuted
clandestinely from England. Had one not the feeling that such things
are so commonplace here, one would say it were material for a book.
I can say honestly that I have met no-one whose family has not suffered.
Simply and well brought up girls, with all the restrictions enforced
on a continental heune fille up-bringing behind them, will tell you
calmly of the hours they have spent completely stripped in a cold
bath in front of eight German officers interrogating them. If you meet
a young married woman at a party, you can ne sure that her husband
is in/prison camp in Germany; everyone is incredibly brave and
no-one complains. Indeed, their only complaint is that they were
not able to do more.

I insist that you all read these words seriously, because I
know that thede stories are true. The Belgians of all the little
nations of Europe are suffering from a terrible inferiority complex,
which is aggravated by their defeat in 1940. The story of their
resistance must be spread abroad so that they may feel proud of themselves
as indeed they should. My attempt to get off a serious note seems
to fail.

I have met a few unexpected friends: Lindsay Mackie, who was
a friend of Richard Timewell and Craven Hohler at Stanstead, is a
Major in the R.A.S.C. at 21 Army Group H.Q. We have unfortunately
met too seldom but long enough for me to know that he, no soldier
by choice, had some harrassing experiences during the landings in
Nromandy and in the sunsequent campaigne. To him the comfort of
a bare room in Brussels was a sort of paradise. I have also met
Franzi de Hass, and Austrian who is married to a Belgian. He
painted Didi ffrench's picture in London before the war, where he
was a great friend of Anne ffrench. Although his wife is a
member of a great Belgian family, the Overstraetens, and they live
in a charming house in Brussels and have the run of the chateaux
of the various members of the family spread out through Belgium,
he is most unhappy owing to his nationality and leads a very retiring
life. I also met Penny Peal, a sister of Jane Nahun, an old friend
of Jebber's. She helps to run the Malcolm Club, which is a great
centre of R.A.F. activity in the town. We met at a party given ny the
Duc d'Ursel, who lives in a large rambling house in the middle of
the business quarters of Brussels. It was built in the sixteenth
century, but has an eighteenth century facade, It is known, quite
rightly, as the dirtiest house in Brussels. The big entrance is
guarded by an incredible old male concierge in blue overalls and a
Dickensian muffler, who showed us upstairs, through a freezingly
cold hall, to the one room they manage to heat. The Duc is a sort
of Belgian Lord Berners and aptronises the Belgian surrealists.
Heshowed me with great pride in one of Francis Rose's better pictures

Red
crêpe shirt

plain back to
shirt

"Red Herring"

4

We have been to some charming parties in the country at various chateaux and large farms. A retired official from the Port of Antwerp living in the country, a widower with two young daughters, gave us a magnigicient dinner and showed us some of his fine Flemish furniture. Some large armoires he had completely altered inside so as to make cachettes for arms dropped by parachute ready to distribute amongst the neighbouring farmers. The farmer showed us his haystacks, which were completely hollow inside and where meetings of up to twenty leaders of the Secret Army had been held. These are only some of many examples.

I went to see a woman, the wife of a miller, one of whose three sons was killed in 1940, whilst another had escaped to Engladn, had been parachuted back into Belgium during the occupation, only to be arrested by the Germans, never to be heard of since. She was living in the house of her third and married son as the mill, which had been the home of the family for 150 years, had been blown to pieces by the Germans as it stood next to a bridge they had destroyed.

Brussels itself is not much changed, except that it is full of troops. The trams are so full that people stand on the steps and often sit on the front buffers. The cinemas are showing mostly old American films of before this war, The few newer films, such as "Desert Victory" and "In Which We Serve" are always sold out. The theatres on the whole are admittedly bad. Brussels depends so much on Paris, but permits for Parisian actors are not granted. The Monnaie is always crowded, but if the prima donas get by, the minor roles and the chorus are bad. You can get a good stall for 35 francs which is the price of a cup of coffee. Incidently, the history of a cup of coffee would make interesting reading. It is made of "Malte" and real coffee, the real coffee having been smuggled up from Spain over the Pyrenees and through France and hidden during the occupation. As regards books, cheaper editions of the classics are almost impossible to find and new books almost unobtainable. Brussels, is however, reprinting a few best sellers like Duhamel and Gide. Even the most intelligent are reading avidly translations of rather trashy English novels, such as "Gone with the Wind" and "When the Rains Came", just because they are English. English papers are still unobtainable on the kiosks, which is the cause of much comment and adverse criticism. Belgian newspapers can only reproduce the B.B.C. as regards war news and are charged with Belgian internal politics.

I cannot resist saying a word about the fashions. There are two great influences at work; firstly among the more sophisticated smart women of about thirty; these, of course, get their clothes from Paris for from Paris influenced Belgian houses. Their clothes are wholly delightful and their hats a triumph. These are truly resistance hats. Their historical equivalent is the large hat of about 1830; they are truly large, that is to say, large crowns rather than brims and are decorated with great complicated bows of brightly coloured silks. Tall and complicatedly draped turbans are also seen. They were worn with deliberate bravado throughout the occupation to cause the maximum of annoyance to the German and his dowdy wife; this object achieved, they are now being modified to suit our more austere eyes. The other influence which is found amongst the younger generation, is that of the "zazou". I do not know where this term comes from, but it is Parisian and means roughly "pansy ruffian". You only see the female variety here. It is sort of romantic, unbalanced, jazz demonstration. The zazou shoe has a high wide heel like a surgical boot with an upper like a sandal and is nearly always made in coloured cloth as leather is scarce; the zazou stocking is made of white cotton, thickly knitted and coming only to the knee, the exact equivalent of the Austrian variety; the zazou skirt is full and unesthetically short, displaying to much bare knee; the zazou jacket is too long for the short skirt and is sometimes cut like a box jacket; zazou hair is just an untidy, long bob, crowned with an

Pale blue
heavy crepe -
silk fringe
& silk embroidered
buttons

Black
over
black &
white
check

172.

enormous hat made of cheap felt, often with a large crown sweeping
up off the face. The true zazou always carries a tightly rolled
umbrella. You can imagine how incongruous is the whole effect, but it is
worn quite seriously on the streets. To tell you how much influence
this costume can have, I can tell you that the heroine and her confid-
ante in "Lakme" wore a tropical version of it in white linen against
the trappings of late Victorian India, without so much as a rousing
smile, except from one member of the audience. O think I am right in
saying that it is jazz romanticism; jazz is going through a revival
here owing to the unbalanced state of mind and very importantly
because the younger generation has been deprived of it throughout
the occupation. I am told that there are male versions to be seen
in Paris wearing tight trousers, showing a lot of brightly coloured
sock, very long scanty jackets and hair down to the shoulder; a sort
of aggressive virile and unbalanced display of resistance.

        After all this cold reporting, I must send a personal word to
you all. Although we sork seven days a week quite hard from nine to
six, having lunch in the Mess together and talking shop (we have
spread it abroad that we do not accept invitations to lunch as they
take up so much of the day) and although none of us really has more than
one night a week to himself as we have to attend so many functions
which are semi-official and semi-duty, we have all enjoyed tremendously
our stay here. All of us, I think, have worked hard with the Belgians
during xxxx the past three years and more, and perhaps it is a reward whi
which I hope we at least partly deserve. It has been a tremendous
experience which I hope you have shared a little from this letter.
One last word, I has been staggering and almost embarrasing to see
what a tremendous prestige the British enjoy here. I only hope that
we shall be able to live up to it.

                    Affectionately always,

                         Hardy.

"ZAZOU"

Brussels '44

This was both a joyful and a sad time. Agents were sought out to be rewarded, Hardy attended requiem masses for the slain and was generally well received. Reunions were held with Hardy as guest of honour and on 5 November 1944 'M. Le Colonel Amies representant la 'Special Force Mission'' was present in Mons, where Britain was thanked and he in turn thanked all those responsible for distributing funds to the resistance, especially agent 'Dingo'. (*Journal de Charleroi 7* November, 1944)

Officially, he was described in his report on 31 March 1945 as 'attached to the Belgian Sûreté to provide (a) long term agents for Germany, and (b) short term agents for infiltration through the lines for the German Directorate. Also liquidating affairs relating to SOE operations in Belgium during the occupation. He has done a good and competent job. He has been the object of some prejudice on the part of some of his Belgian opposite numbers, but has exercised considerable restraint and patience in dealing with this difficult situation...the only criticism... is that he is apt to be impetuous and accordingly he needs a measure of supervision.'

This barb relates to the autumn of 1944. Lee Miller had arrived from Paris as accredited war correspondent and followed events unfolding in Brussels. She mentioned and photographed several people, including an unrecognisable Lt. Col. Hardy Amies patting a dog in a dog cart. He had received the local censor's clearance to cooperate with her. The subsequent report into his role begins quite reasonably, but nastily turns into a snide attack on him. Hardy was accused of promoting his career at the Army's expense – something he had so far been encouraged to do by the Board of Trade for national purposes. In any case, the war was already over as far as his own role was concerned.

'I think I made a mess of this last part of my relationship with the Belgians. I know I was in a difficult position... It was in some ways one of the most difficult and unhappy periods in my life. I made many genuine and lasting friendships in Brussels...We were very near the fringe of the skin-saving collaborationist circle, not to mention the opportunists. More difficult, and

An exercise in flying the British flag: the 'Made in England' suit showing the selvedge on the revers was made for the American film actress Mildred Shay popularly known as 'The Pocket Venus', to wear on her journey to London with her British husband Geoffrey Steele. He joined the army whilst she lived at The Savoy.

Mildred Shay in the 'Made in England' Hardy Amies suit, seated with John Garfield and Geraldine Fitzgerald. Her husband Geoffrey Steele stands behind her, in uniform. 1940.

even touching, was the attitude of the agents we had trained in England. They had been youths at the outbreak of war, and some of them from the most modest homes. We had taken them and taught them to be thugs: in some cases they had become minor stars and heroes, and now we were proposing that they should go back through the Belgian army to a humdrum existence. No wonder we were surrounded by an atmosphere of intrigue and often resentment. I must confess that I left Brussels with a tiny touch of bitterness in my heart. I did not think that I had made a success of any of my work there.'(*JSF* p.104)

Part of the coolness he encountered relates to a feeling amongst many in the Belgian Resistance that their severe losses must have been the result of faulty security within T–Section headquarters or its liason. However there were sadly plenty of traitors within their own country.

He attended his investiture as Officier de l'Ordre de la Couronne by The Regent in the Royal Palace, Brussels. Hardy's cover as a dress designer had been perfect. Undoubtedly his abilities and self-assurance caused some hackles to rise. Gubbins' reaction to Hardy's prize-winning clerihews, appearing regularly in the pages of the *New Statesman*, would no doubt have been uncomprehending incredulity. For example:

The Night Scented Stock
Wears a poor little frock
It was never meant
To be more than a scent.

or

A whiff of Molyneux 'Five'
Helps to keep alive
The myth that there
Was an avant guerre.

and finally

A gigot of mutton
Should have a button
Of garlic neat
Placed where the meat is most sweet.

'Gad, sir!', as Colonel Blimp would have said, and no doubt many of Hardy's superiors did.

Right: *Hardy Amies enjoying a quiet moment, forgetting the war at home in Chesham Place, Belgravia. Early 1945.*

Opposite page: *The rebirth of fashion and the look of 1945, following the end of the war. The spring collections hinted at the shape of things to come.*

HARDY AMIES: suit and overcoat in checked
Otterburn Tweed.
BIANCA MOSCA: wool dinner dress in Jacqmar's
"Sadler's Wells" print.
VICTOR STIEBEL: black wool afternoon dress,
apron skirt and shoulder details outlined in
black velvet.

Chapter Four

CREATING HARDY AMIES LTD

Hardy Amies

Creating Hardy Amies Ltd

During the war most of Hardy Amies' creative talent had been concentrated on his SOE work. Design formed a minor part of his existence, an occasional release and also perfect cover. His pocket diaries reveal that he was in touch with the fashion world, meeting Edward Molyneux, Victor Stiebel and Digby Morton, as well as Charles Creed. Like Amies, their designs adapted naturally to government restrictions and their shared philosophy of 'less is more'.

Amazingly, Hardy's business ticked over with Board of Trade backing, and he pooled resources with Stiebel and others to share staff and rented premises at Worth London's Grosvenor Street building. He had discussed postwar employment with the Worth manager Colonel Pay, then planning a merger of the Worth and Paquin businesses, but Amies would have been submerged again under another name and so he decided to take the colossal step of forming his own House, but to paraphrase Jane Austen: 'It is a truth universally acknowledged that a young designer in possession of a good *clientele* must be in want of capital.' This was not the only problem.

There had already been unpleasant back-stabbing at the end of Amies' army career as a result of war correspondent Lee Miller's innocuous article (and photograph of Hardy patting a dog) in the March 1945 issue of *Vogue*. This incident now had even further dire repercussions for him. Whilst waiting to leave the army, and fearing he might be sent back into the military service, his pay was suddenly stopped. His superior officer, Mockler-Ferryman, interceded as late as 28 June 1945 and staff pay was reinstated, a note in the file stating 'I consider this officer has been hardly treated... Staff pay should not be cancelled'. Amies later wrote, 'I felt mentally exhausted by the struggles at SOE'. (*JSF* p.107)

The promotion of exports was all important to a financially exhausted nation. Amies had proved his economic worth, and the Board of Trade backed his return to England. He finally left Belgium on 28 March 1945, arriving in England by sea on 30 March for a short rest before returning to London life. He met his sister Rosemary, dined with John Fowler at Claridge's and with actor Michael Redgrave on another night, before returning to Leaders for a long weekend. Back in London he met Lilian Hyder, the secretary of INCSOC, went to the Board of Trade to discuss his business plans, met potential backers and suppliers and began designing his next collection. His pattern of life was re-established.

Left: *The Hardy Amies House at 14 Savile Row, in the late 1940s, now restored to its pre-war condition externally and modified within. Built as part of a development in 1735 by Lord Burlington, before the war it had been the source of elegant Parisian fashions, bought expressly for copying from the best French couture collections by the owner, The Hon Kay Norton, who had modern workrooms installed in the building. A tailor occupied the ground floor.*

Below: *Hardy Amies was taken to see 14 Savile Row by the antiquarian Geoffrey Houghton-Brown, a friend of John Fowler and Alexis ffrench, for whom Houghton-Brown also discovered Messing Park in Essex, his country retreat of the late 1940s. The fact that 14 Savile Row had at one time been the home of playwright Richard Sheridan was an additional bonus for Amies, reminding him of his earlier school stage triumph in* The Rivals.

Opposite page: *The revived eighteenth-century staircase at 14 Savile Row, leading from the ground floor to the first floor showroom, which runs across the front of the building. Regularly featured in fashion shoots, it has the unusual feature of a window, opening from the small room connecting the back and front of the house. This is where the playwright Sheridan is said to have sat and observed the entrances and exits of his creditors at the end of his life. (Watercolour by Kenneth King, 1947)*

On VE Day (8 May) Hardy gave a dinner in his flat and then joined the crowds (which included HRH Princesses Elizabeth and Margaret) to cheer outside Buckingham Palace. The next day he dined with Nina Leclercq, John Fowler and Geoffrey Houghton-Brown, antique dealer and saviour of historic houses. This was significant: Houghton-Brown took Amies to see the derelict premises of 14 Savile Row, which would eventually become the centre of the Hardy Amies empire. In time Fowler would decorate it and Leclercq would set up the ready-to-wear boutique. But in May 1945 Hardy was still not released from his military duties; he was officially still on leave until the end of the month, and he returned to Special Forces HQ until 30 June, when he was sent on leave again.

On 3 July he decided to take 14 Savile Row, finalising the lease in October. He had visited Brussels on 17 August to be entertained for some days by former agents, including 'Socrates' and had been invested with his Belgian decoration by the Prince Regent. On the day of his return he had dinner with John Fowler. He was now almost free from SOE. He met Liddell-Hart, as he had a number of times throughout the war, for a form of debriefing, then left for a tour of the Scottish and Cumberland textile mills before arriving at Intelligence Corps Depot, Wentworth Woodhouse, Yorkshire for his demobilisation or 'DEMOB!' as his pocket diary gleefully records on 18 September 1945. He later wrote that the best bit of this was being issued with a superbly made mackintosh.

To Hardy.
With best wishes from
Kenneth King 1954

Hardy Amies Ltd
14 Savile Row.
The Staircase & Landing
formerly owned by Sheridan.

The 1940s evolution of the Hardy Amies overcoat. Top row, left to right: from his 1946 opening at 14 Savile Row 'Eminence' black wool coat with wide shoulders, nipped waist and fuller skirt accentuated by important pocket detail; Amies' 'Romantic Line' of March 1948 evolved from Dior's 1947 'New Look' – a mahogany wool coat with gored skirt and shawl collar lying flat or buttoned high to carry through the single undulating line of buttons; a coat of green/yellow 'new marzipan shade' wool worsted with smoky mother of pearl buttons. Bottom: a coat in the new tent shape, in black velour lined with violet silk. 1948.

A soft Cumberland tweed coat from March 1949 in gun-metal grey and pale blue. The cleverly designed skirt, cut straight and on the bias, suggests a coat and skirt at the back with buttoned belt detail. Wide shoulders offset by large frame collar. The culmination of the Hardy Amies at Lachasse designs for a plaid suit with bell-shaped skirt of 1939 seen on page 56.

Right: *The loosening of the line: a 1950 relaxation of the Amies 1939-40 barrel silhouette in a window-pane check with large buttons. The stand-out pockets reflected in the cuffs with faux flaps and a large shawl collar, and once again accessorised with a long-handled umbrella.*

Opposite page: Hardy Amies: *from his spring collection of 1949, an overcoat of cerise Yorkshire wool with a full-skirted soft-pleated front over horsehair stiffening and two vertical concealed slit pockets to the side seams; two pleats to the back; the full shawl collar here seen flat to the front was intended to be worn rolled under on the wearer's left side. Graduated double-breasted metal buttons accentuate waist and bosom. At this stage, Amies was already giving prominence to his signature as a logo in the silk crêpe lining, fully visible as the coat was removed in a theatre or restaurant, for example. (© Victoria and Albert Museum, London)*

Overleaf, left: *A superbly cut enveloping camel-hair winter sports travelling coat epitomising the best of Amies tailoring, the exaggerated width of the revers an echo of mid-1930s styling, and here given a new twist by the flared line beneath the waist accentuated by the slant of the pockets. Worn with a jaunty ocelot hat. (Cecil Beaton/Vogue © The Condé Nast Publications Ltd.)* Right: *'Neck and Neck' Wenda Rogerson wearing the great Amies' success of spring 1949 in chocolate and white tweed, buttoned to the right and lined with white taffeta. The large collar could be arranged in subtle ways. This was a bestseller in north America, especially for Bullocks Wilshire, and featured in the Anna Neagle technicolor film Maytime in Mayfair. (Vogue © The Condé Nast Publications Ltd.)*

VOGUE

London Collections

Fabrics

MARCH 1949
PRICE 3/-
THE CONDÉ NAST PUBLICATIONS LTD.

Creating Hardy Amies Ltd

Evolution of Hardy Amies suits in the 1940s following the immediate post-war export collection of 1946.

Right: the trim fitted lines of 1947 emerging from a capacious coat.

Below: padded wide shoulders, nipped waist and long jacket over a softly pleated skirt.

Opposite page: 'Fore and Aft ' a suit from Amies' March 1949 spring and summer collection. Grey-toned worsted with black, white and red stripes, with a notched cut-away detail to the jacket echoing the lapels, four metal buttons and large pocket flaps. The soft pleating to one side also to the back in typical Amies style. (© Victoria and Albert Museum, London)

From now on the pace of life quickened further. Meetings with fellow designers Peter Russell and Victor Stiebel all related to the establishment of his own House at 14 Savile Row and the problems of severe post-war restrictions in building materials, fabrics, labour – in fact, everything to do with running a successful couture dress business in London, not least when French couture was already well into its postwar stride.

Luckily the Savile Row landlords were prepared to take a very low rent for the first two years in return for the rennovation of the premises at Amies' expense. In the face of a dire shortage of all building materials this was no small matter. But business licences were eventually issued to Hardy Amies Ltd in the expectation of promoting the name of Britain overseas, employing British labour in various ways, and hopefully drawing in foreign currency. Hardy devised yet another clerihew, based on the President of the Board of Trade, which he used in his press handouts for spring 1946:

Sir Stafford Cripps
Lips
Reports we must
Export or Bust.

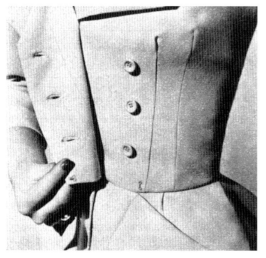

Above left: *An innovative use of a nipped false cut-away jacket over the flared shape of its base incorporating pockets. Circa 1947.*

Above right and opposite page: *Inventive details in tailored Hardy Amies suits of the early 1950s. Above: the ultimate statement in lapels above a pencil skirt, the velvet collar reflecting the New Edwardian style in men's clothes, also seen opposite in a skin-tight sheath of a suit featuring triangular-buttoned pocket detailing. (© Norman Parkinson Ltd/Courtesy Norman Parkinson Archive)*

Left: *A detail of the opening of an Amies jacket, illustrating the imaginative design of a tightly-fitted jacket translated into form-fitting and retaining tailoring. Circa 1947.*

Lady Pamela Berry at Hardy Amies, circa 1952. Married to an owner of the Daily Telegraph, she was a highly social and an effective President of The Incorporated Society of London Fashion Designers (INCSOC) of which Hardy Amies was a founder member in 1942. Both were the subject of a Nancy Mitford 'tease' in the Daily Express during July 1959, concerning the state and quality of London couture, which she denigrated. Some thirty years later at a lunch in New York, they joined forces again in an attempt to convince the Duchess of Windsor to bequeath her jewellery to the Victoria and Albert Museum.

His small trading capital was initially derived from his stepmother, Mary Amies, and augmented by his client Lady Jersey, Alexis ffrench, his father and later in April another client, Mrs Montagu Meyer, amongst others. Miss Linton of Linton Mills also bought shares in the company and showed her trust, as did other textile companies, by extending credit to a man who had proved his worth as a viable business proposition. John Fowler began to decorate the building in the most effective and cheapest way possible, 'Child, you must remember this house needs weight. You must give up all attempts to make these beautifully proportioned rooms look like a dress shop.' And so on Monday 12 November 1945 Hardy and employees moved in.

It was a tightly run operation, staffed by a manager E.R. Fothergill (ex Belgian SOE), two existing Lachasse sales staff 'Cammie' (Miss Campbell) and Violet, Victor a Czech tailor, and from Worth a very fine Swiss fitter named Odette, soon followed by most of her workroom; they were augmented by youngsters to be trained, including a number of refugees.

Left: *Suits into day-dresses, the button-through fine wool skirt and bolero jacket creates a rounded slender profile. It was the antidote to the earlier full-skirted Amies 'Romantic' style, cleverly focussing attention on the belt and blouse. in 1951, the year in which the Hardy Amies Boutique opened. Below: an antecedent displaying all the restrictions of austerity regulations from 1945, the hat size providing the balancing note for the proportions of the design.*

Creating Hardy Amies Ltd

Hardy Amies evening dresses of the post-war period are lessons in cut and construction closely allied to the type of materials which inspired them. Top left to right: the slender silhouette of 1946, long sleeves and typical asymmetric draped bow at the back; a hip-hugging backless satin sheath from 1949, draped into a full skirt of contrasting colour, the culmination of his 1939 designs. Below left to right: button-through elegant simplicity with a belt above two off-the-hip pockets, circa 1947; a draped and gathered belted satin top flowing into angular planes, posed on the landing in 14 Savile Row, circa 1950; a pleated neo-classical sheath with applied tie details to the neck and waistline, circa 1949.

Opposite page: Hardy Amies considered Norman Parkinson to be the consummate photographer of his designs, always capturing the mood and elegance Amies intended to convey. A ballerina-length pleated silk dress and evening coat heightened with a single flower, a Molyneux touch that Amies admired and copied. (© Norman Parkinson Ltd/ Courtesy Norman Parkinson Archive)

Left: *Journalists and buyers usually concentrated on the tailoring of Hardy Amies suits and coats, but he was also an inventive designer of evening and day dresses. Seen here is a gathered draped full-skirted taffeta evening dress with a bustle effect displaying his pre-occupation with the back as well as the front of the design and here also concluding his pre-war ideas.*

Opposite page: *Vital publicity in the editorial pages of a 1950 magazine indicating the new Amies models and materials used in clothes illustrated in the preceding pages. The sketch of the coat refers to the image on page 86.*

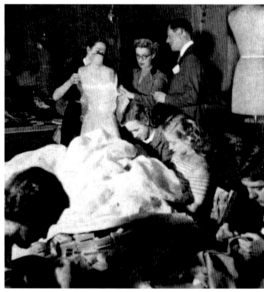

Right: *A favourite image of Hardy Amies working with Maud Beard (left), a fitter who began her career with Miss Gray Ltd and having known him since he was two years old remained a link to his mother. 'Cammie' stands next to her. (Photo: Chris Ware)*

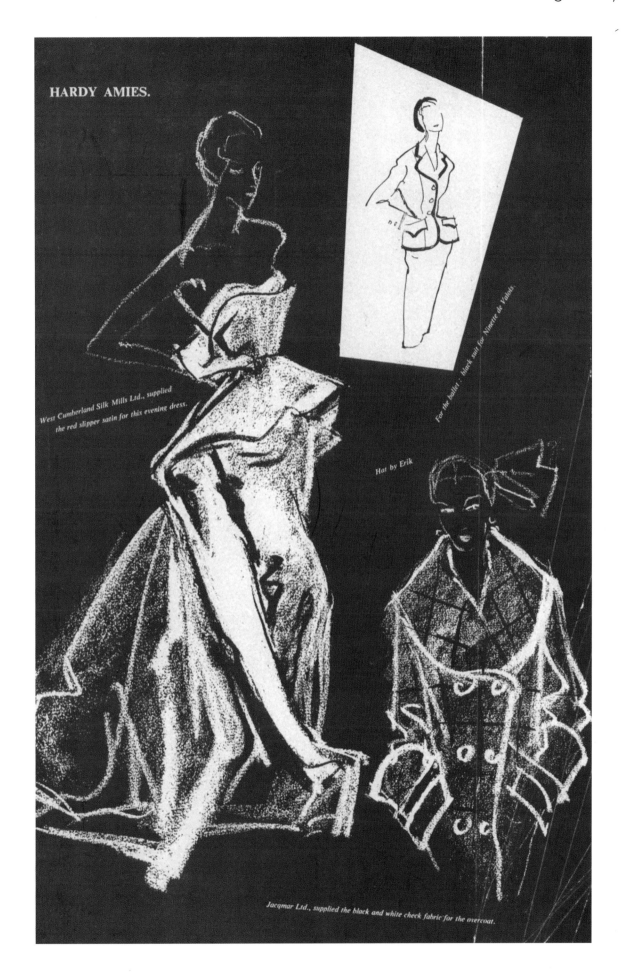

HARDY AMIES.

West Cumberland Silk Mills Ltd., supplied
the red slipper satin for this evening dress.

For the ballet : black suit for Ninette de Valois.

Hat by Erik

Jacqmar Ltd., supplied the black and white check fabric for the overcoat.

The sheer fabrics utilised in these three designs inspired a fluidity and softness not usually associated with Amies. Right: the ultimate tulle over a 'Romantic' style silk crinoline, created for a young girl at a time when debutantes were still a fixture in the London social calendar, circa 1950. Bottom left: a finely pleated evening coat with wide draped sleeves, circa 1949.

Opposite page: A stiffened, pleated, tiered crinoline with an overlay of fine lace and accentuated with a cape and an oversized voile tie, reminiscent of the famous dress for HM Queen Elizabeth II (see p.163) circa 1952. (© Norman Parkinson Ltd/Courtesy Norman Parkinson Archive)

More orders flowed in than could be dealt with: department stores Marshall Field of Chicago and I. Magnin of San Francisco placed theirs before the first show on 28 January 1946, when the felt floor coverings were still being laid as clients walked up the stairs.

So began the re-establishment of Amies' valuable links with the USA, a relationship that carried on until he gave up business. Later in the year, he set out by air for Marshall Field in Chicago to participate in their first post-war showing of English and French clothes, having first visited New York and Pittsburg stores. The show was a success and he visited Detroit, New York meeting his friend Virginia Jersey, and then on to Boston. After two weeks he was home with open orders to send £8,000 of clothes selected by him from the next collection. He was made.

Right: *Mid-century Hardy Amies timeless feminine elegance highlighted by London Vogue in March 1950 with the caption, 'Great allure in a short evening dress with a corset-tight bodice of white guipure lace; hip swathed, back-sashed skirt of navy-blue figured silk. (A lace collared bolero makes it a cocktail suit.) Erik cartwheel.' Amies chose this image for his second autobiography, Still Here in 1984. (Don Honeyman/Vogue © The Condé Nast Publications Ltd)*

Opposite page: *The advent of the short evening dress, rarely seen since the 1920s. A black satin strapless tiered sheath under draped coin-spotted tulle, this is a version of the dress photographed by Norman Parkinson which featured as the cover of London Vogue in March 1950, with the caption, 'Tulle stole drifts from huge bow. Buckled pumps by Rayne. Lentheric lipstick Rocket Red.' (© Norman Parkinson Ltd/ Courtesy Norman Parkinson Archive)*

Right and below: *'Green Dolphin' suit in French rayon: a slight loosening of the line in winter 1949. Worn with one of the hats (below), the only three shapes used in this collection.*

Opposite page: *Classic Hardy Amies in 1947. A love of stripes and of striking designs, using them in unusual ways was an established part of his style by 1939, expressed most boldly here in a ballerina-length dress with a cutaway wrap-over skirt, tied at the waist with a crossover bodice in his 'Romantic Look', influenced by Dior's 'New Look', admired by Amies. Without the wrap-over and in varying lengths, the silhouette endured for more than a decade. (© Norman Parkinson Ltd/Courtesy Norman Parkinson Archive)*

During successive seasons, Amies astutely built on his core workforce and fostered the growth of his domestic and export business. He was a consummate showman. Appearances on early television shows were augmented by his participation in BBC broadcasts and a continual flow of interviews given to the press, overseen from 1946 to 1949 by Heather Burn, a friend of Virginia Jersey from her wartime days living in Richmond, when she 'adopted' a Polish flying unit. Heather eventually married one of the pilots, as did Virginia on her divorce in 1946 from Lord Jersey, who had been financing another INCSOC member, Bianca Mosca.

In February 1947 Christian Dior launched what became known as his 'New Look'. Almost overnight, other styles became outdated, dowdy or just too reminiscent of the war that people wished to forget. Freed from the restrictions imposed on British suppliers and consumers, French fashion captured the headlines. The INCSOC members responded with many clothes of extraordinary distinction, interpreting the French mood, not just slavishly following it and offering much in the way of elegant style and good craftsmanship, appealing not just to British clients, but also to large numbers abroad. It was a form of business warfare and Hardy Amies relished it.

Chapter Five

FOR QUEEN AND COUNTRY

Hardy Amies

SECRETS OF FASHION—No. 5

The man who once sold weighing machines for a living and now designs some of the world's loveliest clothes is described here by **LILIAN HYDER**

Lilian Hyder

Hardy Amies

Behind the scenes at Hardy Amies Savile Row Salon

Hardy Amies (centre) talks with two of his models while Mr. Ernest, the tailor, adjusts a hemline

The Amies Touch. Tailor Mr Ernest perfects a hem-line on a model, whilst another enjoys the fun, circa 1950.

Previous page: The swansong of the stunning, fashionable winter coat. Hardy Amies, framed by the middle window of his main showroom (he disliked 'salon'), looks down to scrutinise Bronwen Pugh in tweed, winter collection 1959-60. Evolved from Amies' 'Pyramid Line' of 1946, it acknowledges Yves St. Laurent's influential 1958 'Trapeze Line'. The inset plaque commemorates Sheridan's tenure, and reminded Amies of his schoolboy acting prowess. The striped blind was based on one at his childhood home in Alperton, London.

Few dress designers can claim to have influenced fashion more than once in their careers, if at all. Hardy Amies had a small effect on the design of women's suits in the later 1930s, but until he re-invented his career in the 1960s with menswear, his influence was more persistently one of interpreting current trends for a sophisticated clientele, not necessarily very rich, at home and abroad.

His influence was boosted after 1951, as a potential designer to the young heir to the throne HRH Princess Elizabeth, who placed a small initial order, which resulted in success for Hardy Amies Ltd, and publicity in the illustrated press and newsreels for the forty-year-old designer. Writing of the forthcoming 1947 marriage of the Princess, he predicted, 'November 20th will be the birth of the Elizabethan era. When we have a queen on the throne, women and fashions will follow the trends set by her.' (*Globe & Mail* 15 October 1947) This indeed came true, as Queen Elizabeth's choice of dress became a source of global interest from then on.

Amies' postwar success was neither unwarranted nor unexpected. He summed up a consistent design philosophy concerning his bespoke clothes: 'An understated look of clothes is associated with this country. All the British upper classes look like they have come up from the country to London. We are not an urban race; we are a country race that goes to London for fun.' (*Going Strong* p.20)

As *Vogue* stressed in January 1947, 'His soft woollen dresses, suits and coats are a perfect foil for Englishwomen, but he is really in love with the dinner dresses and *robes d'interieur* which he does so well.' His clientele at home responded with all the enthusiasm their ration books allowed. When asked by an American what the coupon allowance could buy in one year, he replied, 'two suits and a girdle' and he told a Canadian, 'An average suit takes over four yards of 54" material for which we receive only 18 coupons, the same as a suit of less material.' (*Montreal Daily Star* 10 October 1947) His 1947 collection statement stressed the dearth of cloth used for one model and the necessary substitution of another for copies. Such was 'Austerity Britain', whilst across the Channel in Paris, Dior's influential 'New Look' lavishly utilised all materials with no government restrictions, and the French couture houses reaped the rewards.

From dawn to dusk: the unified look of a mid-twentieth-century collection, displaying the full talents of each workroom as they applied their skills to Amies' inventive designs. A perfect example of his oft-quoted statement that he absorbed French trends without slavishly following them. Circa 1950.

Left: *The Amies transition from the 'New Look', which he had begun to detest because of the untidiness of the flapping and bunching of skirts between the legs. The shoulder-line of the loose thick coat is now much softer, and the coat, lined with the same silk as the thin wrap-over dress has an interior pocket. The coat is also visible far left page 109 and represents the Amies evolving 'Princess Line'. Circa 1951.*

Below: *The Amies 'Princess Line' of the early to mid-1950s, the coat given distinction by furred cuffs and pocket flaps to the buttoned design, all evolved from his 1940s designs. Circa 1953.*

Amies' export business grew. Americans liked his designs, although attempts to establish new markets in the Commonwealth met with difficulties. Fashion editor Alison Settle reported in February 1947, 'the United States is making a determined bid for the Australian market and UK fashions are hardly known, their cost quadrupled by import duties'. (*Observer* 4 February 1947) This explains Amies' regular trips to north America from 1946, unceasing until the 1990s.

A pioneering spirit was needed by foreign buyers viewing the 1947 spring collections in London. 'During the big freeze-up, bundled in fur boots, warm jackets and warm but unattractive hoods, we shuffled into the luxuriously-decorated salons of the haute couturiers to see their export collections'. (*The Queen* 19 March 1947) By December it was reported, 'Hardy Amies knows where he is going. The most serious and ambitious of

Transition to the 'Swinging 60s'. Top left: a buttoned coat with pared fullness to the soft silhouette utilising an established Amies envelope-pleated skirt, narrow cuffs to three-quarter sleeves and slim stand-up collar balanced by wide hat. Circa 1962. Top right, an abstract print dress and matching loose coat for summer, circa 1964. Bottom left: winter coat fullness with deep pockets, three-quarter sleeves and tie detail to the collar, circa 1962. Bottom right: the mid-1960s country look of a loose tweed coat, the waistline detail caught by the complimentary design of the simple three-buttoned high-necked suit with tiny pockets and worn with a country hat. Circa 1964.

Hardy Amies' inventive suits reflecting the finest British cloth and tailoring. Below: a tiered belted jacket detailing above a full box-pleated skirt, circa 1950. Right: a buttoned velvet suit with nipped waist emphasised by pocket details and notched hem over a pencil skirt, circa 1952.

Opposite page: Soft tweed, sleek tailoring, the quiet pocket lines reflected in the backward flare of the off-centre rear skirt panel. A look as refined as the Comet passenger jet aircraft seen in the background. Winter 1950-51. (© Norman Parkinson Ltd/Courtesy Norman Parkinson Archive)

all London designers, he has made a successful bid for the American market ...his clientele are mostly under forty.' (*Strand* December 1947) American store Henry Morgan announced, 'Amies is the creator of suits which have ushered in a new era of feminine tailoring. The test of a good suit... [is that] once put on it should be possible to forget about it for the rest of the day.' (*Tailor & Cutter* 28 May 1949)

In 1948 Lady Olivier, international star Vivien Leigh, was pictured 'buying heavily' at Hardy Amies. Subsequently, they became good friends. He also hosted an in-house show of 'dateless designs' by the mercurial New York-based designer Charles James. 'James is one of the most brilliant research workers in that field of artistic endeavour known as dressmaking' Amies said in an interview with the *Evening Standard*, and James returned the compliment, 'In England there is an extraordinary renaissance in design... possibly more apparent to the visitor than to the resident.' James was then

From workroom to fashion plate, the perfect fit of Mr Ernest's tailoring skills with an eye-catching asymmetric line to the buttoning and pockets, enlivened (left) by posing in front of the 'dog-tooth' architectural capping to the granite of Westminster Bridge steps. Circa 1951.

the most expensive dressmaker in the world. Amies was duly photographed sitting on the floor at the packed showing. Behind the scenes Amies and his cutters examined the intricacy of James' famous tailoring, reflected in two Amies evening dresses of this period now in Bath Fashion Museum. They reveal just what Anne, Countess of Rosse meant, when she wrote that it took a 'considerable time' to work out how James' creations should be worn. (*The Genius of Charles James*, pp.93, 111). Growing royal patronage after 1951 solidified Hardy Amies' status.

Careful not to flaunt this, and adept at warding off intrusive questions, the commercial benefits were soon capitalised on by his old friend Nina Leclercq, who forsook Paris *Vogue* to set up the Hardy Amies ready-to-wear boutique, an affordable attraction for those wanting the glamour of the Amies name without the full expense. Amies and Leclercq visited the Schiaparelli and Dior boutiques in Paris, also those already in London of

Easing the line. Right: a loose jacket over a simple buttoned blouse and plain belted skirt circa 1959. Far right: a tweed winter suit with dropped shoulder line, large collar with doubled faux tie, the tapered skirt loosely gathered at the waist, circa 1961. Below: a summer suit with the tied neck of the blouse showing through a short jacket with button details above a slim skirt with slight fullness to a gathered waist. Circa 1961.

Creed, Digby Morton, Mattli and Worth. By the end of 1951 Nina Leclercq had visited America with an extensive ready-to-wear collection of suits and coats priced at US $100-120. (*Vogue Export* no. 4 1951) Success was echoed at home in the society pages of *The Tatler* which reported 'Miss Leclercq, Hardy Amies and his new co-director William Akroyd at a Belgravia charity dance hosted by Mr Alan and Lady Patricia Lennox-Boyd.' (*Tatler*, August 1951) Hardy Amies the dressmaker, was a celebrity and now socially acceptable, as Britain moved into a more egalitarian age.

Often called a snob for the wrong reasons, Amies never disowned his modest origins. In December 1951 he returned, as he often did, to Brentwood and opened the Settlement Bazaar. At such an event he could observe and absorb the needs of real women. He signed a contract to produce exclusive designs for the housewife readers of *Woman* magazine in 1951, whilst designing show-stopping couture dresses for clients such as the concert pianist Eileen Joyce, and observing the 1954 Café de Paris performances of Marlene Dietrich, who graced Savile Row in the year he published his first autobiography, *Just So Far*. Following a celebratory dinner at home to launch the book, one guest wryly commented in his visitors' book, 'It's far enough.' If Hardy saw the comment he ignored it,

Left: 'Quorn' and 'Pytchley': the Amies interchangeable tweed suit, a shorter skirt with bold box pleats beneath a boxy double breasted jacket, the same jacket worn over slim tapering matching trousers. The concept was applied to a knickerbocker suit for his most lavish client Lady Delamere and is clearly inspired by Amies' menswear designs of the period. Circa 1964.

Below: A draped loose jacket with lavishly fur-trimmed cuffs and collar, over a slim dress with flat-buttoned bodice detail to the left above the softly gathered waist. Amies loved designing seductive day and evening clothes, but they rarely made headline news for him. Circa 1962.

and continued to be photographed with stars like Maria Callas and Benjamin Britten, summing up his ongoing love of opera, the stage and celebrity, not least his own.

Yet, Amies kept his feet firmly on the ground. He knew he was fallible: 'There is a beast in every collection. I get no satisfaction whatsoever in designing something that doesn't sell... I have every respect for the public taste, my customers are always right.' (*Maclean's* 1 June 1952) He was also diplomatically forthright with clients. Linda Christian wanted a square-shouldered suit like that of her husband Tyrone Power, but Amies refused, 'We can't have you going out of here looking like a boxer.' That 1940s look had gone and he paraphrased Chanel's theory, 'Every fashion is a child of a fashion before. We can only expose so much of the human figure and from time to time we change the display.'

1950s daytime sophistication in London. Top left: 'Cross Currents', an elaborately draped and gathered bodice, the detail over one shoulder apparently emerging at the slim waist as a sash pocket detail, 1949. Below left: the flutes of a Rolls Royce radiator complement a pencil-thin day dress with draped and gathered detailing to bodice and waist, circa 1950. Top right: a coin-spotted silk day dress with three-quarter sleeves and wide bow to the open neckline. Circa 1950.

Opposite page: Termed 'A Little Late-Day Dress', now known as a cocktail dress, one of a group in black rayon jersey with long sleeves and a high neck to the front, falling as a loose cowl in soft folds behind. Small hat with cockade by Vernier marking the end of the fashion for bare heads in the evening – for a time. Photographed at the entrance to the old West India Docks on the Isle of Dogs, 1952. (© Norman Parkinson Ltd/Courtesy Norman Parkinson Archive)

Amies proved his interest in 'changing the display' (and demonstrated financial acuity) by designing the new uniforms for the waitresses or 'nippies' of Lyon's Corner House restaurant in Leicester Square in 1955, the year he was granted a Royal Warrant.

By October 1957 his diversity was evident. His designs for HM the Queen had brought him free worldwide publicity, and the evolving sophistication of his Amies' style was expanding his business, 'I am working to capacity and turning away orders. My workrooms of 200 can turn out about 2000 garments a year, but I am actively limited in output by finding those who can sew, and even if I could find them, where in Savile Row am I going to put them? Handwork is dying out here and will eventually disappear as it has in New York... As I can't expand my couture business, I devote much of my energy to my ready-to-wear business, as I hate to be static.'

Opposite page: *The Hardy Amies look of the early 1960s: a selection of blouses from the Hardy Amies collections sold in the ready-to-wear boutique and modelled by Sue Lloyd (top and bottom right).*

Above: *The end of the 'Princess Line' and 'Little Late-Day Dress'. A short evening dress of flowing chiffon, finely gathered on the bodice and worn with a voluminous long stole. Circa 1963.*

For Queen and Country

Previous page:

Left: *The mid-century style of a Hardy Amies full-skirted evening dress. Crimson satin with a v-shaped arrangement of shoulder straps from a loose flat-draped boned bodice, running into a large puffed bow at the back, echoed in the soft folds and bows to each side of the dress. The full shape is maintained by a possibly experimental lining of man-made Vilene, a stiffening fabric, rather than more usual elaborate underskirts. Although keen to use fabrics of natural fibres, Amies was not alone in constantly experimenting with new manmade materials. Circa 1950 (© Victoria and Albert Museum, London)*

Right: *Hardy Amies in his showroom with 'Hope', one of his most successful designs. A strapless full-skirted organdie evening dress with bands of white Nottingham guipure lace, with a buttoned long-sleeved white lace jacket. Spring and summer collection, 1950. (© Norman Parkinson Ltd/Courtesy Norman Parkinson Archive)*

Opposite page: *By the mid-1950s Hardy Amies was established as 'Dressmaker By Appointment to Her Majesty Queen Elizabeth II'. This dress of burgundy tulle with flocked velvet spots typifies the fine detail and craftsmanship used in the Queen's clothes. The fashionable full skirt falls from a slightly dropped waist of layers of alternating burgundy and white tulle over a vermillion taffeta underskirt. Wide shoulder straps and crossed detail of the bodice are in tulle with interlaced satin ribbon tied in bows. As is usual with many such dresses, the bodice is silk-lined over the boning.*

Left: *Hardy Amies reveals his love of women en grande tenue. A voluminous short-sleeved velvet evening coat with draped back and trimmed with fur over a full evening skirt suitable for a Royal Gala at Covent Garden, circa 1952. An even more elaborate version was shown at the Mansion House in 1956.*

Far left: *A dress for a grand entrance in two colours; the crossover gathered bodice held by one shoulder, and tied at the waist with a puffed bow above the diagonally gathered full skirt with integral train. Circa 1962.*

Left: *Hardy Amies reflects transition in fashion. A dramatic version of a Paisley print draped from the waist in gathered folds to the back and with long bell-shaped sleeves set against art of the period.*

Opposite page: *The Amies youthful romantic style in a setting epitomising his own vision of British timeless aristocratic elegance. The deceptively simple outline is derived from a complicated structure concealed by an elaborately gathered tulle bodice and multi-layered ballerina-length skirt, flowing into a long train. Circa 1956.*

Above left: *An updated version of the 1950 success 'Hope' shown on page 123, and (centre) an unusual twist with a scatter-pattern to the dress and a plain border to the skirt. Both circa 1962.*

Above right: *The long and the short of it in the early 1960s. A short evening dress and coat at The Royal Opera House, Covent Garden. A boned bodice for the strapless dress with deep-gathered detail, accentuated by a large flower on the waist ribbon, above a two-tiered skirt.*

For Queen and Country

Right: *Showing Hardy Amies collections in-house, spring and summer, circa 1961.*

Opposite page: *Hardy Amies with two evening models in the showroom at 14 Savile Row, from the mid-1960s. The large Pucci-type print on the left indicates the loosening of form, as does the skirt and jacket on the right. Increasingly preoccupied with menswear and the international merchandising of his name, Amies was often away for many weeks or months and Kenneth Fleetwood was virtually in charge of all designs for women. Amies would usually comment on and select from his designs, then inspect and criticise the finished clothes, before they were completed and shown.*

Amies continued, 'Anyway, in designing it is economical. I can only repeat a model in my couture collection twenty times, but in the following season adapt it for ready-to-wear and hundreds of repeats. I design for a set purpose: to make clothes for English women suitable for the life they lead, and for foreign clients with the same tastes. If I put models in my collections just to give the press girls something to write about I would be in Queer Street.   I have to change every one of my models twice a year. Imagine Ford cars doing that! As far as I can see, our couture will continue for the next twenty years much as it is now.' (*The Queen* October 1957)

This perceptive and typically optimistic view of the future was made in the knowledge that the darker days following the death of George VI in 1952 were long gone. Amies now had light and hope for the future, not least through the work of Kenneth Fleetwood, his talented protégé, who was becoming an accomplished designer and remained with Hardy Amies until his untimely death in 1996.

Below left: *Amies with one of his most faithful clients, Lady Dartmouth, now Raine, Countess Spencer. Circa 1958.*

Below right: *A charity show at Belvoir Castle with another loyal client, Margaret, Duchess of Argyll, her daughter the Duchess of Rutland, and son Brian Sweeny. Circa 1962.*

Chapter Six

KENNETH FLEETWOOD IN HOUSE

Hardy Amies

Kenneth Fleetwood: In House

Previous page: *Garment patterns stored in the Hardy Amies archive, housed in the former workrooms at Hardy Amies Ltd, 14 Savile Row in 2010. (Photo Toni Ryan)*

Above: *Kenneth Fleetwood MVO (1930-96) in September 1963 with one of the Amies dachshunds. Joining Hardy Amies as a sketch artist in 1952, by the early 1960s the protégé was designing most of the womenswear collections, albeit under the eagle eye of Hardy Amies.*

Below: *Once asked what he did when not working, Ken mischievously replied, 'I like to sleep a lot'. Enjoying a snooze in Cornwall, where he and Amies often took holidays to plan collections, sketch, and entertain friends, here in the company of the quintessentially British actor Michael York, who together with his wife Pat became friends of Hardy and Ken. (Photo courtesy Pat York)*

By 1952 Hardy Amies Ltd was expanding. In addition to a growing number of couture customers, the Boutique, American and Canadian export orders and the patronage of Princess Elizabeth all guaranteed large orders and increasing publicity. Amies was already a familiar participant on radio and television programmes and had appeared on television before the war. His face was increasingly that of a celebrity, and he lived like one. His full engagement books show a regular pattern of life emerging. Tennis lessons, skating lessons, Italian language lessons, weeks abroad on business, or away sketching his collections, holidays such as his 1951 month in Italy during which he and Alexis ffrench dined with Sir Henry 'Chips' Channon and Peter Coats, skiing holidays, opera at Covent Garden and Glyndebourne, racing at Ascot, tennis at Wimbledon and always office appointments with models such as Barbara Goalen, photographers Norman Parkinson and Cecil Beaton, and actresses such as Edith Evans and Constance Cummings, who were dressed both for the stage and off it. His whirl of activity was very occasionally interrupted by a couple of days, laconically noted in his diary as 'Ill in Bed'. As early as 1947 the business had extended laterally into the upper floors of 15 Savile Row, 'As the seasons went by, it was quite evident that the house was as full as an egg.' (*JSF* p.138)

From conversations with fellow designer Edward Molyneux and his own observations, Amies knew the value of a good assistant such as Edward Molyneux's John Cavanagh, who opened his own House in 1952. About this time Amies met the young designer, Kenneth Fleetwood, then studying with the Australian artist and stage-designer Loudon Sainthill. Amies was

Two of Fleetwood's vivid lightning sketches produced after observing members of the Royal Family at a Covent Garden Royal Gala performance in the 1980s.

Fleetwood was adept at sketching from an early age, and could quickly give an artist's impression of what he or Amies had in mind for a design. This sketch dates from his days at St Martin's School of Art and indicates his empathy with Amies' own ideas circa 1950.

Kenneth Fleetwood: In House

Fleetwood discussing matters with tailor Mr Michael, with Women's Wear Daily *open on the desk, 1959. The Wigan-born designer, known for his dry Lancashire wit, often said that he had first been employed at Amies 'picking up pins', but from the first he was intended to assist and support Hardy Amies in the design and supervision of the processes involved in creating couture garments, learning from the skilled employees at 14 Savile Row.*

Opposite page: A Kenneth Fleetwood silk evening dress, circa 1970. The spotted crêpe bodice with long sleeves, and the printed organdie overskirt over white, with a tasselled rouleau belt. By the mid-1960s Fleetwood epitomised the Amies style and designed the collections, whilst Hardy mainly oversaw the emerging designs and completed clothes. This dress belonged to a friend and early client of Amies, the fashion journalist and historian Ernestine Carter. (© Victoria and Albert Museum, London).

impressed by Ken's sketches, knowledge and enthusiasm at their first meeting, and a friendship began, only to be ended by Fleetwood's death in 1996. Ken was knowledgeable about art and music, Hardy about opera and life in general, and both shared a passion for couture. The younger man was equally accepted by Rosemary, and as the years went by Ken was established as one of the family.

There is a parallel with Hardy's earlier educative friendships with Jonny Witte and Alexis ffrench, even with his contemporary John Fowler, who called him and many others 'child', even though he was only three years older than Hardy, but Fowler was much more scholarly. For example, he gave Hardy a copy of the highly detailed *Life in a Noble Household 1640-1700* by Gladys Scott Thomas, with the inscription 'To dearest Hardy with my love for Christmas from John 1943'. Thirty years later Hardy displayed his own interest in the seventeenth century through the design and furnishings of his Oxfordshire house, decorated in conjunction with Colefax & Fowler. It is often assumed that Hardy and Ken had a long and intense physical relationship, but this was not the case. When Alexis ffrench died of cancer in 1956, Hardy was deeply affected, and Ken undoubtedly came to fill a void in his life.

Kenneth Fleetwood: In House

Ken's upbringing in dour 1930s and wartime Wigan included observations of his own mother, a skilled tailoress, making clothes at home; his father worked for the Ince Wagon Works. Eight-year-old Ken was bright, winning a school prize for making a full toy stage, whereas all the other children copied that of the local Rex Cinema. He also won a BBC *Children's Hour* competition. His parents encouraged his educational interests and those of his sister; the ENSA wartime travelling dramatic and ballet productions fired his imagination and on leaving Wigan Grammar School, a visitor to the end of year art exhibition on seeing Ken's work was so enthusiastic that he repeatedly besieged the Principal of St Martin's School of Art until Ken was accepted as a student. According to his sister, Ken showed no emotion or surprise at this. (*Author interview with Margaret Brown, 2011*)

After leaving St Martin's in 1951 and his short spell in theatre design, Fleetwood remained with Amies until he died – apart from National Service in 1953. Asked in 1989, why he had never left, he typically said that he had considered it twice, but preferred being at Amies. (*MOL* 1989 interview) Ken shared a flat off Notting Hill, so run-down that one of the occupants kept a motorbike in his room. A mutual friend, the decorator Kenneth Alexander Partridge, was appalled by Ken's poverty, and urged Hardy to pay him more. During his National Service Fleetwood had been ill and suffered liver damage, subsequently neglecting his strict diet, so Hardy's housekeeper fed him and he was given a room in Hardy's house.

Above: *The young protégé's passport photograph of the 1960s, in later years a source of agitated confusion at the airport, as often packed at the bottom of his bag.*

Right: *Neil Roger, known as 'Bunny' injected capital into Hardy Amies Ltd. Known as a pre-war designer and formerly based at Fortnum & Mason Ltd, he moved his small business and workforce to the Sheridan Room of 14 Savile Row, in what had been Amies' own office to the right of the entrance.*

Opposite page: *Hardy Amies at the 1960s wedding of the daughter of his highly valued company secretary Stanley Cox, who joined the firm after the war and remained there until his retirement. Flanked by two of the most important women in his life, Nina Leclercq (left) a pre-war friend, who set up and managed the Boutique, and his sister Rosemary, to whom he remained very close throughout his life, and who worked for Hardy Amies Ltd for fourteen years as the personnel and administrative manager.*

Left: 'When a saleswoman says to the stock-keeper "I want some steel grey satin, pure silk, fifty inches wide," she must know where to get it. She has two indoor assistants and two outdoor assistants called matchers ...I work in very close contact with the stock-keeper when I am buying for the collections.' (JSF p.192)

Below left: On working holidays with Fleetwood in a rented Cornwall house belonging to Anne ffrench's family during the 1960s, and which was also a favourite holiday destination for Ken Fleetwood's sister and her family, Amies would use the break to discuss the forthcoming collections. The PR image belies the reality, as Amies rarely sketched designs himself after the mid-1940s.

Below right: 'Which comes first, fashion in cloth or the fashion in clothes? ... I hate all fabrics which attempt to master me... patterns that can only be used one way up... bold stripes and checks that have to be manipulated in one way only... bordered fabrics, for the border has to be established first and the dress cut up after that.' (JSF p.234)

Opposite page: Hardy Amies at seventy in 1979 with (left) Miss Lilian, the Queen's fitter and head of the workroom. Just visible behind her head is Joe, a tailor in Mr Michael's room, and third from left is Ruby a general assistant, or 'hand'. Sitting on the table (behind Hardy) is Nancy, a trainee tailoress in Mr Roy's room, and Lynda known as 'Little One', a tailoress in Mr Michael's room is also present. (© Norman Parkinson Ltd/Courtesy Norman Parkinson Archive)

Above and opposite page: *Fittings for the autumn/winter collections of 1959, Amies scrutinising every last detail of a woollen suit featuring the higher jacket with the larger buttons fashionable at that time and (right) examining the look and structure of a heavy overcoat worn over a loose dress gathered and held at the waist by the fashionable large belt of the moment. Seen here are Mr Ernest, fitting the dress and the coat, and Ken Fleetwood and Mr Michael, seated on the sofa on the right.*

When Hardy moved, Ken then had a self-contained flat in the new house, later buying a nearby flat, but remaining forever chaotic in his domestic arrangements. It suited Hardy to have him nearby and bounce ideas around; they walked from Kensington to Savile Row most days, but for years did he did not appear at Hardy's smart dinner parties. More importantly, nor did he receive any formal acknowledgement as a designer for almost two decades. This is perhaps not so unusual in the couture world, but it was a situation with which Amies might have empathised.

In 1985 Hardy wrote, 'Kenneth Fleetwood is in essence an artist ... by nature a dreamer though with his feet kept on the ground by a strong streak of northern common sense. He is a musician with perfect pitch and has the power of total recall... [he] ...strives to improve and maintain our reputation as designers of originality and taste. His Lancashire blood makes him a shrewd shopkeeper.' (*SH* pp.78-80)

In 1974 Ken was given the title of Design Director, a belated public acknowledgement of his established role, for he had also been designing for the Queen for many years, although not officially until 1982. Amies had just arrived in America when he received a message that the Queen had requested his presence with new designs several weeks earlier than arranged. Ken was accepted in his place and 'the Queen wrote a message saying that she had spent a very happy afternoon.' (SH p.113) Hardy explained his own attitude to his co-designers, 'I am interrupted in all but the most important meetings to be shown models when they are being fitted. This happens so often that by the time the collection is ready on show day I really feel that the clothes are mine.' One can imagine the Amies gimlet eye glinting and the faint sardonic smile, 'I say this not in any way to diminish the skill and devotion which Ken and his team give to their work.' (SH p.152)

The elegant chic of the famous Hardy Amies cut, utilising fine fabrics for a suit (right) with unadorned rounded shape, the jacket with small bows as fastenings and a coat (left) with spotted lining over a neat dress clasped by a large belt with buttoned fringed belt loops running from the bodice. Circa 1959/1960.

The workrooms were so devoted to their appointed tasks that the strict rule of silence, initiated by their heads in 1946, lasted in varying degrees until the end. This rule was usual in couture workrooms. Their concentrataion on work in hand was absolute, and every detail of each couture garment was closely monitored until the perfection demanded by everyone involved resulted in a true Hardy Amies masterpiece of design, cutting, sewing and finishing. Jon Moore remembers the total quiet of certain workrooms, creating an almost religious atmosphere. Soon after his appointment in 1979 he was asked by Ken Fleetwood (who was away ill) to finish the toile of a design destined for HRH Princess Michael of Kent. Hearing that the client was downstairs, he took the toile away to show it to the client and vendeuse. He was met with stony glances and left, and was later forcibly told by the vendeuse never to repeat such behaviour, and then had to explain himself to Hardy Amies. Upstairs workroom hands seldom, if ever, went to the sales floors, and entered and left the building by the staff entrance. They might know the

Photographed in-house: the Amies-Fleetwood easy style of the mid-1960s pays homage to both Chanel and Givenchy, with minimal detailing to the suits and dresses, relieved by buttons and large bows to the deep necklines. Conveniently light to pack and unfussy for the new era of jet-setting. Circa 1964.

name of clients, but in all other respects, client discretion was an absolute rule that was strictly adhered to by everyone.

The 'team' was augmented by interesting period characters. Lord Teignmouth was one of the best sketch artists Amies ever had in the late 1950s, subsequently involving himself with Hardy's menswear. Money, always the biggest problem of any couture house, was put into the company by two friends of Amies: Neil Roger, known as 'Bunny', a son of a rich self-made Scotsman, who could never quite believe his son's unnecessary career as a dress designer, let alone his unabashed dandified appearance and glamorously louche parties. Another was William Akroyd, the scion of a rich Yorkshire carpet manufacturer with capital to invest who also needed an occupation. Both men had distinguished war records and were well-known in London society. They passed a good part of the day at the Amies House, often in the Sheridan Room, formerly

Couture chic in Swinging London: two Amies-Fleetwood overcoats and a suit, deceptively simple lines concealing the tailoring of fine materials, devoid of most decoration in the Amies manner, excepting fur cuffs around high wrist- lines. Circa 1966.

Hardy's glorious office decorated by Fowler and ffrench, and subsequently Neil Roger's showroom for his floating creations which were most often sold to friends of his mother or, if more practical, to younger married women friends. They often bought from the Amies collections instead, as in common with most couture houses, there were in-house models and daily shows at set times. Akroyd was consulted by Amies on business matters and supposed to look after the staff, however the enduring memory of one contemporary is of him busy with the crossword, smoking in his 'office', a sort of hut in the courtyard at the back, or simply chatting with clients. (Geoffrey Angold interview) The ambience of the House and Mayfair at this time is encapsulated in Norman Parkinson's 1950 photograph of William Akroyd amongst 'The New Mayfair Edwardians' outside 14 Savile Row.

From the ultimate simplicity of mid-1960s Amies-Fleetwood evening dress design (top left), to the late 1960s nod to Flower Power with palazzo pants (bottom left), via the more formal feather-trimmed dresses of the mid- to late-1960s. Circa 1967.

Kenneth Fleetwood: In House

A small-checked coat worn over a suit with a central panel cut on the bias emphasised by buttons (far left); louder checks used in a suit with black fur trim and hat (left), alongside a similar check used for a hat and checked suit, worn under a short coat with tie belt. Circa 1967.

The first sight of the Art-Nouveau revival of the early 1960s, seen in a summer silk coat worn over a plain dress and topped with a dashing upturned wide-brimmed hat. Circa 1963.

Moving with the times, a tweed mini-skirt worn under a loose matching cape with a form of blanket edging and contrasting buttons circa 1969; the short lived maxi-length given a horizontal twist by Fleetwood circa 1972.

Opposite page: The Amies couture version of the Yves Saint-Laurent peasant or 'gypsy' fashions of the early 1970s in a dramatically patterned dress and long headscarf. Circa 1974.

The shapes of the 1980s into the 1990s: the rounded wider form of an unadorned brown-toned tweed coat and dress with a belt (left) contrasts with the vibrant pillar-box red of a full, belted dress with a touch of black and full three-quarter sleeves gathered at the cuffs.

Ken Fleetwood 'hated the horrible 1970s – very bad for couture. The 1980s brought renewed interest'. (*Museum of London interview, 1989*) In 1979 Jon Moore joined the business as an assistant. Born in 1957 and trained at Kingston, he is of a far younger generation than Fleetwood, and was taken on for the future of Hardy Amies, then the only substantial couture House remaining in London, albeit with a seventy-year-old-owner and an ageing workforce. As a portent, the extra space previously needed and taken at number 15 in 1947 was then being vacated, and the design studios, including those for home products, were dispersed. Nevertheless, collections were made and shown, and Moore adapted to the idiosyncrasies of the people and the building. Amies was often away in America, Australia or the Far East with Roger Whiteman attending to the large licensee business.

By the late 1980s Moore was appreciated for having contributed much to the evolution of the Amies line for women's clothes, making it more

seductive, not least, because he can and does cut and sew himself, formerly a rare gift amongst dress designers. Hardy could hardly fail to notice and in 1985 commented, 'His considerable charm is of great value in dealing with the customers.' (*SH* pp.78-79) Moore was of considerable value in many other ways to the business, not least in arranging the updated seasonal fashion shows and accompanying Fleetwood abroad on buying trips for the ready-to-wear clothes subsequently given a Hardy Amies label and sold in the Boutique.

The evolution of fashion at Hardy Amies circa 1990: the full softly pleated skirt of the suit is reminiscent of the 1940s, the loose unfitted jacket and the tie of the blouse a homage to the style of the mid-1960s.

Right: *Fleetwood-Amies late 1960s sophistication: the countrified style of a blue-and-white checked evening dress lifted by ruffles to the bodice, sleeves and skirt, suitable for smart outdoor dining and dancing in warmer climes, reflecting the winter migration of the Amies jet-setting clientele. Circa 1968.*

Opposite page: *Kenneth Fleetwood and Hardy Amies revisit the past with a novel twist to this early 1990s revival of the fitted suit, displaying elements of pre-war styling in the shoulders and drape of the sleeves, and reviving the post-war shape in the jacket worn over a looser long skirt and finished with a dashing brimmed hat by Frederick Fox.*

It was at this time that Ian Garlant, also with a Kingston education, joined as a studio assistant for womenswear. When the menswear designer left, he was asked to take on the job. For the next ten years or so until Fleetwood's death, the life of the House went on season after season with recurrent financial blips. Garlant and Amies shared many interests, including music, literature and opera. He also got on well with Fleetwood and was sometimes invited for weekends at the Amies country house.

Kenneth Fleetwood: In House

Kenneth Fleetwood at 14 Savile Row with three of his evening dresses of the early 1990s, the original sketches of each design can be seen on the floor. Each reflects a facet of Hardy Amies designs of the early 1950s to early 1960s. The early sketch by him (page 133) displays the same concept for an asymmetric skirt, an idea that clearly stayed in his inventive mind.

Australian-born Frederick Fox was already a well-known London milliner when Hardy Amies first asked him to design hats to accompany his collections in 1968. He designed five hats to accompany Amies' designs for the Queen, worn during State Visits to Brazil and Chile in 1968, the first of many during the following three decades. He was granted a Royal Warrant in 1974 and his hats were also worn by Queen Elizabeth the Queen Mother, and later by Diana, Princess of Wales. He was appointed LVO in the Queen's Birthday Honours of 1999. (Tim Graham/Getty Images)

Hardy Amies outside 14 Savile Row with a model wearing a bouffant Fleetwood dress over tight trousers inspired by Eastern costume, a variant of the image especially photographed for the dust jacket of Amies' second autobiography Still Here, published in 1995. (© Norman Parkinson Ltd/ Courtesy Norman Parkinson Archive)

153

Above left: *Jon Moore, the first of the two talented designers to work with Fleetwood from the 1970s, and who did much to create a more fluid interpretation of the Hardy Amies style, here fitting a svelte evening dress in the showroom at 14 Savile Row in the early 1980s.*

Above: *Le rouge et le noir; his and hers by Jon Moore wearing his own design in the staircase balcony at 14 Savile Row. His first solo show was for the spring/summer collection in January 1996. He was Women's Wear Designer 1986, Couture Director 1989, Design Director 1996-2001 and left in October 2001 to set up his own company.*

Left: *White draped jersey evening dress with wide shoulders and lace sleeves, the detail of the back openings a 1979 revival of an established Hardy Amies design by Jon Moore. Known as 'Columbia' the gold and black version of the design was named 'MGM' by Ken Fleetwood.*

Opposite page: *Dramatic red satin chiffon evening dress: a Ken Fleetwood updating of a neo-classical design, reminiscent of another symbol of British excellence, the Rolls-Royce bonnet mascot 'Spirit of Ecstasy'. Circa 1993.*

HARDY AMIES

Amies seemed to find a reflection of his young self in Garlant, once referring to him as his 'grandson', a title also bestowed on members of the younger ffrench generation. Ultimately, Garlant summed Amies up as 'a good actor' and now considers him to have been 'the most egocentric, self-centred and compelling man I ever met, and I've met a few' adding 'I also loved him'. (*Author interview and correspondence, 2012*) Part of the

---

Above left: Jon Moore introduced a more overtly sensual line to many of his designs, as seen here in this black evening dress with sheer lace side panels from autumn/winter 2000.

Left and above: A navy blue and white striped dress, an Amies classic combination, as is the coin-spot suit with a long jacket, both with the shorter skirts echoing the mini-skirt, increasingly fashionable again in the 1990s.

Ian Garlant at Hardy Amies revisits the designs of sixty years previously with a heavily gauntleted coat with large collar (left), and a suit with parti-coloured tweed jacket with cuffs. 2006.

disillusionment of both Garlant and Moore must lie in the fact that Amies announced plans for the continuation of the business to be left in trust for the staff after his death. This became impossible for him to achieve. Sadly for everyone, his assets were in property and a pension fund; his bank statements reveal a modest salary and income over the years. His couture business became increasingly uneconomic, although Jon Moore can point to the business latterly making a profit when he was the designer. Although bolstered by licensing income, the financial demands were insatiable, and ultimately overwhelming as London rents soared. As long as he could, Hardy clung to the building and bolstered the prestigious couture. The Hardy Amies name still financed and supported his lifestyle with the Royal Warrant maintaining kudos and continuing business. With age came physical restrictions: no more tennis or skating; skiing long in the past; no more long walks. Garlant noticed that his quick mind remained, and now fuelled a growing impatience: he bored easily. (*Author interview*) Had he retired, he would almost certainly have been quickly ignored, with few of the parties and invitations that filled his life after the deaths of both Ken Fleetwood and his sister Rosemary, whom he never thought to outlive.

Hardy Amies and some of his staff on his eightieth birthday in 1989 in the showroom of 14 Savile Row. As is evident, he inspired both respect and affection from his workforce, and most of them remained loyal to him for many years.

Sir Hardy Amies in white tie with miniature decorations seated beside his assistant designer, Ian Garlant, who became the designer under the new ownership of Hardy Amies Ltd in 2002.

Ian Garlant witnessed Amies' reaction to the news of his knighthood in 1996, 'I've done it.' Overnight, he seemed to adopt the character of a sage, and an authority on what was done or not done, which led to some unfortunate quotes in the press, as when he pronounced the Queen's white shoes to be in bad taste, but it was his own lapses into bad taste that caused his reputation to suffer. He was not safe alone with journalists, as Peter Hope Lumley discovered. Selina Hastings was with him at a theatre, when he loudly pronounced the dress of a woman nearby to be 'naff'. (*Author interview with Selina Hastings, 2012*) This comment was not atypical, but can be seen as a manifestation of grief and is not uncommon. He missed his sister and Ken, and now had too much time time to dwell on past sadnesses including his suppressed SOE experiences and the terrible fate of so many agents of the Belgian Section. *The Times* obituary of Belgian Resistance hero Gaston Vandermeersche on 21 November 2010 mentions his belief at the time that there was a double agent at work in T-Section. Amies never discussed details of this painful episode in his life.

After the departure of his press secretary Heather Burn in 1949, he employed Peter Hope-Lumley, a nephew of Molyneux, to do the work. Lumley (whose telegraphic address was LUMLUGS) was to be his faithful public relations agent for the next fifty years, as valiant a struggle at the end as in the beginning with his new client. After a few months of penury, he asked for a larger fee. An argument followed and Amies was accused of being 'mean and grand'. Amies shot back, 'mean... but I have no money so I have to be mean. Grand – I suppose I am grand, but then I have so much to be grand about.' (*Museum of London interview 1989*) They remained lifelong friends.

Opposite page: *Hardy Amies at eighty in the showroom at 14 Savile Row, the carpet and chair cushions woven with his geometric monogram, and the catwalk covered with sketches of designs for his favourite client, Queen Elizabeth II.*

CHAPTER SEVEN

QUEEN ELIZABETH II

Hardy Amies

Previous page: *Her Majesty Queen Elizabeth II in the White Drawing Room at Buckingham Palace wearing the Hardy Amies dress worn at the State Banquet at Schloss Augustusburg, Bruhl, during the State Visit to the Federal Republic of Germany, 1965. Amies based his design on the blue and white Wittelsbach colours of the early rococo interiors he had seen on his visits in the late 1920s. The embroidery was executed by S. Lock & Company. (© Cecil Beaton/Victoria and Albert Museum, London)*

Above: *By Royal Command. Leaving Savile Row for a fitting at Buckingham Palace in 1954. Left to right: vendeuse Betty Reeves; dressmaker Maud Beard; Hardy Amies; tailor Mr Leonard; the Amies doorman with well-concealed clothes and one of the younger workroom staff, increasingly in short supply even then.*

Opposite page:
Top: *Queen Elizabeth II in the Throne Room of Buckingham Palace in December 1952 with her Prime Minister Mr Winston Churchill, during the Commonwealth Economic Conference. Six premiers and two finance ministers, left to right: Mr D. S. Senanayake (Ceylon); Sir Godfrey Huggins (Rhodesia); Mr Holland (New Zealand); Mr Menzies (Australia); Mr Havenga (South Africa); Mr Khawaja Nazimuddin (Pakistan) and Sir Chintaman Deshmukh (India). Six months before she would wear her famous Coronation Dress by Hartnell the Queen wore this impressive Hardy Amies three-tiered full-skirted crinoline of light mauve Swiss organdie cotton with white embroidery which had been designed for her 1952 Tour of Australia, postponed due to the death of King George VI. It clearly pleased the Queen, who wore it again at a reception given by the London County Council at County Hall on 6 July 1953 and subsequently during the Royal Tour in February 1954 at the Civic Ball in Hobart, Tasmania. (Fox Photos/Getty Images)*

Below: *The Hardy Amies sketch of the evening dress prepared for HRH Princess Elizabeth in 1951 to be worn during the cancelled Tour of Australia in 1952 and subsequently worn as HM Queen Elizabeth II.*

In 1950 Hardy Amies received a visit from HRH Princess Elizabeth, the heir to the throne, and her sister HRH Princess Margaret. Norman Hartnell was then the sole designer for Queen Elizabeth, consort of King George VI, although her daughters had lightened Hartnell's workload for the 1947 Royal Tour of South Africa by including clothes designed by Edward Molyneux.

Amies wrote that he received the Princesses in his downstairs office, where they were shown the latest collection. (*SH* pp.84-85) On Monday 5 July 1951 at 4.45pm he noted his desk diary 'Lady Alice Egerton & Princess Elizabeth' and on Saturday 14 July at 10.00am (after a haircut at Claridge's) a car took him with some designs to Clarence House, where the Princess and her husband the Duke of Edinburgh lived. This is the first record of visits to the Princess, who succeeded as Queen in February 1952, and is subsequently seen in Amies diaries over five successive decades. 'How proud I am that I have been and still am able to serve the Queen by making dresses for her... To me Queen Elizabeth II typifies all that I admire most in the English women's attitude to dress', he wrote in 1954. (*JSF* p.243) 'Everything was relaxed, but totally businesslike.' (*SH* p.85)

Canada 1951

no fur.   No 7

Delivered 21.9.51

Canada 1951
No 1

3/4 Length

Delivered 21.9.51

Beard

cut

Australia 1952

6R
Beard cut

White gaberdine
overcoat

Australia 1952

Cut.

Delivered 28.1.52

Turquoise blue
trimmed
phantom beaver

1954

Colour &
material

SUGGESTION FOR MATERIAL.
COLOUR AS IN SKETCH K.

SKETCH J.
Overcoat in bright cherry wool, with soft important collar
of phantom beaver. To be worn over matching thin wool dress
(sketch K).

Hardy Amies' first designs for Princess Elizabeth included these coats for the Royal Tour of Canada in autumn 1951 (opposite page, top left) cut on the 'Princess Line', as were two intended for Australia in 1952 (bottom left). Instructions to the workrooms are visible, as with the cherry-red coat (left), made in 1954. Below: A velvet coat adorned by 'The Maple Leaf Brooch', the diamond brooch given to the Princess's mother Queen Elizabeth during the Royal Tour of Canada in 1939, worn here in Quebec in October 1951.

Amies ascribed the royal interest in his clothes to the sight of them being worn by one of the daughters of his client Countess Ellesmere, Lady Alice Egerton, a new lady-in-waiting to the Princess, although many others within sight of both princesses and the Royal Family were already clients. Several members of the Royal Family were present as Caroline Margaret Montagu-Douglas-Scott, the youngest daughter of the 8th Duke of Buccleuch, married Ian Gilmour on 10 July 1951 in an outstanding Amies wedding dress. The fashion and daily press were full of reports on Amies and he was never reticent in giving his opinions on clothes.

The first 1951 designs worn in Canada were considered successful; the press reported that Amies' designs matched the requirements of his client. Hartnell sent him a congratulatory letter, and the press was told, '...he is very glad to have someone to share the responsibility – and the blame!' (*Montreal Daily Star* 6 September 1951) Their wary mutual regard was cemented during the State Visit to France in 1957, 'it was a very pleasant experience for me to have shared the visit with him.' (*SH* p.99)

Above and left: *The Amies design for the ensemble worn by the
Queen for an afternoon performance in the renovated Theatre
Louis XV at Versailles on 9 April 1957, during the State Visit to
France. In 1996 Amies remembered saying to the Queen,
' "Ma'am, could I do the dress for that because I know the
colouring?" I made her a pale-blue dress with fur at the cuffs.
Wonderful!' (Daily Mail 16 November 1996) The coat of thin-
ribbed watered silk with mink cuffs, with a dress of finer silk
embroidered by S. Lock and Company, in a manner meant to
evoke the dresses of Queen Mary. The day was cold and the
dress remained unseen by the public; weather was always an
unreliable factor in designing for such occasions.*

HARDY AMIES Ltd

Telephone 14 *Savile Row.* W.I. *Regent 0738.*

H.A. 7.
Loose overcoat to wear over dress H.A.6.
The material is a heavy Yorkshire woollen,
woven to match the crêpe of the dress. The
coat hangs straight from the circular collar,
has no fastenings and has cuffs of phantom
beaver on the threequarter length sleeves.

HAT BY KAYE DAY
Close fitting hat in draped electric blue
velvet.

Hardy Amies' evolving coat designs illustrating his comment that the Queen is fashionable without being in the height of fashion. Above: a coat worn for her arrival in Washington on 16 October 1957 during a State Visit to the United Nations, and for a visit to his old school Brentwood, on 30 October 1957; Amies was present at the Queen's request.

Above left: one of several light ensembles worn during the visit to India and Pakistan from 21 January–2 March 1961.

Left: the looser line of fine woollen coats from the early 1960s and waisted line of the mid-1960s, fore and aft.

Left: *Hardy Amies suggested brighter colours and patterns to the Queen, enhancing her visibility in public. Visiting the ailing Duke of Windsor during the State Visit to France from 15 to 19 May 1972, the Prince of Wales accompanied his parents to the house of the uncrowned King Edward VIII, who abdicated in favour of his brother, King George VI, father of Queen Elizabeth II, in 1936. Amies liked the tailored elegance of the Duchess of Windsor's dress sense.*

Opposite page:
Above: *The Queen greeted by Emperor Hirohito (left) in Tokyo at the beginning of the State Visit to Japan, 7 to 12 May 1975. Of the Hardy Amies mauve dress and Frederick Fox hat he wrote: ' "Imperial colours" said the Japanese, "How flattering to us!" I had no idea, but I shouldn't be surprised if the Queen had known.' (SH p.107)*

Below: *The Queen in a red and white ensemble, typical of the bright colours worn by her in the 1970s, here during the 1975 State Visit to Japan, when Hardy Amies was in the country attending to his successful licensing business. He was invited to one official reception.*

It became the practice for Hartnell and Amies to submit designs as ordered by the Queen, apportioned fairly and conveyed to each House, usually by Miss MacDonald, her dresser for many decades. No formal consultation between the designers usually happened and there was healthy rivalry to produce the finest styles, Amies conceding that Hartnell won with the finest of grand embroidered evening dresses. (*SH* pp.99 et seq.)

The Royal Tour of 1953-54 reinforced the Amies capacity to design and deliver suitable clothes, which blended so well with those of Hartnell; the two subsequently designed in tandem. Kenneth Fleetwood at Amies gradually designed more from around 1960 and Ian Thomas, formerly with Hartnell, became an official third from 1970 onwards.

After the grant of the Royal Warrant as 'Dressmaker to The Queen' in 1955, the fame of Amies spread worldwide. The effect on his business was dramatic over the period to the 1980s, when there were forty-eight worldwide licensee agreements in operation, largely looked after by Roger Whiteman, who travelled extensively with Hardy Amies. When the Queen visited Japan in 1975, his licensees insisted that he be there at the same time.

Amies immediately grasped that the clothes he was to design for the Queen should be fashionable, not in the height of fashion. They were to aid the sovereign in what she told him was 'going about her business'. (*SH* p.82) Over the years, with the Queen's consent, he also offered successful models from current collections of day clothes, sometimes with changes, rather than

design exclusive ones. These were suggested with a choice of different materials, only for her. The Amies format of brighter colours and patterns with smallish hats evolved, all to aid visibility. 'A hat is a crown', as he prophetically stated in January 1951. (*Hull Daily Mail* 26 January 1951) The changing length of dresses was always considered, so that no more than a minimum of knee would show in the varied conditions in which clothes were worn. 'As short as we dared', was an Amies note beneath a photograph of the Queen from the late 1960s, when the mini-skirt was fashionable – Amies hated the mini-skirt for couture.

The straightforward consultation process with the monarch, for whom time is very precious, has been described by many and was discussed by him in 1985, 'It has been the Queen's practice to call her dress-makers to the Palace to discuss the clothes needed for a particular tour. This message is usually relayed to us via the Queen's devoted dresser, requesting us initially to go to the Palace with sketches of clothes we intend to propose. A series of fittings at the Palace follows and eventually the wardrobe is delivered to the care of the Queen's dresser, who is then responsible for its packaging and transport on tour.' (*SH* p.96 et seq.)

13.   *H.A. 5.*

Sleeveless dress in navy and white
vertical striped chiffon, with navy
belt. Easy casual coat in crepe de
chine matching pattern of dress, worn
with double chiffon scarf with matching
pure silk fringe edging.

White organza cloche hat with navy
grosgrain band.

Worn during Jubilee tour, England.
Also " " Australia.
Previously worn for arrival in
Philadelphia, July 1976

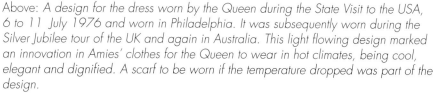

HARDY
AMIES
LONDON

Above: *A design for the dress worn by the Queen during the State Visit to the USA, 6 to 11 July 1976 and worn in Philadelphia. It was subsequently worn during the Silver Jubilee tour of the UK and again in Australia. This light flowing design marked an innovation in Amies' clothes for the Queen to wear in hot climates, being cool, elegant and dignified. A scarf to be worn if the temperature dropped was part of the design.*

Right, top: *The designs for the Queen's coats in the 1970s were often in the style of this yellow fitted design with a slightly flared skirt worn with a matching neat spotted turban by Frederick Fox. The Amies style contrasts strongly with that evolved by Norman Hartnell for Queen Elizabeth the Queen Mother, glimpsed (on the left) in the background. Made for the State Visit to Mexico in 1975, and worn here to view the fireworks display on the Thames in Silver Jubilee Year 1977.*

Right: *The Queen's Silver Jubilee Anniversary Service on 7 June 1977. The design of double-lined heavy silk crêpe withstood the windy steps of St Paul's Cathedral and was worn to the delight of Amies and milliner Frederick Fox, as it had been worn by her as Queen of Canada when she opened the Olympic Games on 17 July 1976 in Montreal.*

4. Blue & white façonné spot chiffon loose coat with pretty sleeves cut on the cross.

HARDYAM

Two summer chiffon designs for the Queen in the spirit of the successful ones worn in the USA and Canada in 1976, with the fuller sleeves of the right-hand design indicating the emerging line of the 1980s.

HARDYAMIES

No 4.
Canada 1951

NO BELT.

D. ..... 21.9.51.

Delivered 23.1.52.

Australia 1952

Australia 1952.

Hardy Amies designs
for suits submitted to
Princess Elizabeth and
approved in 1951. The
slim version was worn
in Canada in the
autumn of 1951. More
orders were completed
featuring the cooler
full skirts in the
Princess Line for the
postponed trip to
Australia and New
Zealand in 1952.
These accomplished
sketches were by an
Amies sketch artist and
show details of the cut

The Amies *vendeuse* to the Queen plus necessary fitters would attend, usually with Amies, later with Fleetwood and latterly Jon Moore who fondly remembers the fortifying cup of tea and two biscuits with which he was supplied. The designers would then sit outside the room until the Queen was dressed and afterwards observe the fit of the clothes. Often the Queen would walk around the room, carry a bag, wave an arm or sit to judge the fit and effect, with the aid of large mirrors in the dressing room.

Amies was also later allowed to take the milliner supplying him, to judge the effect of hats with the clothes, so that a sense of design unity was maintained. From 1968 on this was the Australian, Frederick Fox, who subsequently held a Royal Warrant. It had been Amies' constant gripe that previous milliners Kate Day and then Aage Thaarup had attended the Queen alone, so that hats and clothes were not necessarily working to the same end. This innovation was tested, and clearly worked. Even so, Amies was unhappy if hats were not necessarily worn with the clothes for which they were intended. In much later years, he could be petulant in interviews about the accessories not matching his designs, and evinced a hatred of white shoes and bags on arms, which gave his loyal press officer Peter Hope-Lumley some testing times of his own.

The recorded results of Amies' contributions to the Queen's style speak for themselves, some more photogenic than others, yet all were avidly scrutinised around the world, not least by the designers and their staff. Amies noted in interviews that the Queen herself observed that photographs were often unkind to both wearer and clothes. Usually no prior notification of what might be worn was given, or if a designer was known to have provided something for a special occasion, the details were embargoed until the moment it happened. In the early days, Commander Colville, the press secretary to George VI and then Queen Elizabeth II, kept a fierce eye on any transgressions and was feared by designers and most, but not all, of the press.

Hardy had famously high standards of design and was not immune to self-criticism, as his autobiographies and countless interviews underline. Looking back in 1985 he wrote, 'I count the garments on the fingers of one hand that have been rejected [by the Queen] and more than half of these were withdrawn at my request.' (*SH* p.92) Sometimes things did not turn out as expected, as he described to a friend:

'I have always thought it would be a joy to dress the Queen in black with all the jewels and the Garter – it is sure fire theatre. So I was pleased that way back in the spring of 1980 my request to submit sketches was accepted & fittings followed in due course. My scheme was to use very fine lace over grey, so that dead funereal black was avoided. The Queen seemed pleased and I went off to USA & Queen to Balmoral, returning only a day or so before leaving for Rome (including the Vatican).

The Queen wears an Amies suit in the spirit of the late 1970s with a Frederick Fox hat of the same material as the bodice. Circa 1977.

A Jon Moore-Hardy Amies
design for the Queen in
green silk worn during the
State Visit to Thailand,
21 October to 1 November
1996. The longer jacket
began to replace the coat in
the 1990s and this Amies
design reflects the change,
here also affording some
relief from the heat. 'Weather
is always exceptional', as the
Queen is fond of saying.
(SH p.112) 'The Queen was
so pleased with the ward-
robe we made for Thailand
that her parting words were:
"I'm going to Canada next
year." ' (Daily Mail
16 November 1996)

HARDY AMIES

Opposite page: A Kenneth Fleetwood design for the Queen, of mulberry wool,
worn with a Frederick Fox hat on the Great Wall and accompanied by the Duke
of Edinburgh during the State Visit to China, 12 to 18 October, 1986.

Right: *One of the first day dresses designed by Hardy Amies for Princess Elizabeth's postponed Tour of Australia and New Zealand of 1952. The printed material is given a form of fichu around the sweetheart neckline to the front, and the back given the attention for which Amies was famous, here with a swagged, gathered drape.*

Below: *For the Royal Tour of 1953-54 Hardy Amies was commanded to make a number of ensembles to augment the vast number being undertaken by the established designer to most ladies of the Royal Family, Norman Hartnell. This elegant white lace dress was both cool and fashionable, the effect heightened by the broad-brimmed hat and parasol, the long-handled shape a fashionable accessory of the time.*

Opposite page: *In 1957 the Queen made history when she recorded the first televised Christmas message, twenty-five years after her grandfather King George V broadcast his own first message on the wireless. For the occasion she selected this Hardy Amies dress with a sweetheart neckline above a bodice draped as a bow. As Queen of Canada, in Ottawa, she had worn the dress previously that year, with a small hat by milliner Kate Day.*

HARDY AMIES L*d*
14 *Savile Row.* W.1.
Telephone *Regent* 0728.

H.A. 4.

    Cocktail dress in beige and gold brocade in
a leaf pattern. The full circular skirt is
folded into unpressed pleats. The bodice is
finished with draped bow.

HAT BY KATE DAY

    Draped turban in same brocade as dress,
trimmed with beige velvet.

Chosen 11.6.71
for
Turkey

Left: *During the 1960s Fleetwood and Amies simplified the silhouette of the Queen's day dresses, following prevailing trends. This yellow-and-white checked day dress with tie collar, gathered cuffed sleeves and thin belt above a pleated front was designed to be worn under a matching coat, clasped by a fashionably wide belt with large buckle and the buttons and pocket details of the time. Worn during the State Visit to Turkey, 18 to 25 October 1971.*

Below left: *Accompanied by Prince Edward and surrounded by athletes, the Queen wears a pale pink day dress in Canada, 1976.*

Below right: *A pale draped spotted chiffon dress worn by the Queen for a walkabout in the heat of Harlem on 12 July 1976 during the State Visit to the United States.*

Opposite page: *A Fleetwood-Amies design for a less rigid form of day wear for the Queen, utilising a vibrant black-based silk print, with tiny pockets and a pleated front. Circa 1990.*

Black ground floral print,
Silk dress with bound
pockets and hem.

Opposite page:
Far left: *The Hardy Amies design for a long day dress of black lace worn for the State Visit to the Vatican on 5 May 1961 to meet Pope John XXIII. The full skirt is no longer in the crinoline style of the 1950s.*

Left: *Fleetwood-Amies designs typifying the youthful fashion of the mid-1960s. Three of several designs ordered by the Queen for a dress to be worn by HRH Princess Anne at her Confirmation. Subsequently adopting her own distinctive style, the Princess was only seldom seen at 14 Savile Row.*

Cocktail Dress in mauve lace over lilac chiffon and pale pink satin. The Dress is gently fitted and finished at the hem with the lace scallop and finely sunray pleated lilac chiffon. The ¾ length sleeves are also finished with the lace scallop.

HARDY AMIES

'Imagine my dismay when photo of Queen appeared wearing black velvet dress – quite nice but obviously not ours. (It was by Ian Thomas.) No explanation at all from Palace or Queen herself whom we saw just before and just afterwards. I naturally thought she hated dress or me! So before next visit to fit clothes for visit to Brussels I suggested to Miss Macdonald (sic) that the Queen might like us to alter the dress so she could wear it privately as dinner dress – it meant lowering high neck line. We had, with Queen, commented on what a pretty dress but not gloomy dress it would make. At last visit to Palace the Queen said to my women (me not present) "I can't think why Mr Amies wants to alter my black dress, it's very pretty: not dark enough for Rome. I'm saving it." '(*Letter, HAL Archive*)

Above: *A Jon Moore-Hardy Amies design for an afternoon dress, with separate pleated skirt, the longer-skirted version transferable into a long dress. The latter version was ordered and worn at the wedding of HRH Prince Edward to Miss Sophie Rhys-Jones at St George's Chapel Windsor on 19 June 1999.*

HARDYAMIES

Above: *A blond cashmere suit from the Amies ready-to-wear collection, 1985. The Princess largely patronised and encouraged younger designers, whilst fashioning her own image.*

Opposite page: *Two designs for HRH the Princess of Wales from the early 1980s. The Princess wore a Hardy Amies suit for her official engagement photographs, bought from his ready-to-wear range at a London store. Designs for her wedding dress were requested, made by Jon Moore, submitted and rejected without the identity of the wearer being known by the designer.*

Designing for the Queen and other members of the Royal Family is a magnified extension of designing for couture clients dressing for various occasions.

Top left: Often the bottom of a design is completely obscured so equal attention must be paid to the top, as here behind microphones in the glare of the sun during the Royal Tour of 1953-54.

Top right: The design must allow the wearer to move freely and elegantly even in tricky situations such as negotiating a gangplank as seen here in New York, July 1976.

Below: The Queen is still visible from a distance, wearing a light pale day dress designed by Hardy Amies, and worn during the Royal Tour of 1953-54.

Far left: *The Queen in a red Amies ensemble, the hat similar to the Elizabethan Hartnell design of that worn for the Investiture of HRH the Prince of Wales in 1969. Accompanied here by HRH The Duke of Edinburgh, the design and colour of the ensemble are distinctive in the military setting.*

Left: *Arriving for a hot outdoor engagement and carrying a parasol, the Fleetwood-Amies sleeveless design has a narrow front pleat and is worn with a kerchief hat, typical of the early 1970s.*

Below left: *The Queen with King Taufa'ahau Tupou IV during a visit to Tonga on 7 March 1970.*

Below right: *The chagrin of the client and despair of the designer, when a carefully made dress encounters the unexpected and irresistible forces of nature. 'Weather is always exceptional', as the Queen is fond of saying. (SH p.112)*

Left: *Remaining elegant in the heat of a closed carriage, an Amies design worn in Ethiopia during the State Visit of 1 to 8 February 1965.*

Below: *For the State Visit to Saudi Arabia of 17 to 20 February 1979, Amies designs conformed to the local religious dress codes, and the Queen was suitably veiled for her arrival (below left) in a dark long-sleeved day dress embroidered by Lock with matching head-dress, as well as a lighter-coloured version worn on 19 February for a picnic (below right).*

Right: *The Hardy Amies original design for the dress marked 'Delivered 21.9.1951'.*

Inset: *One of the first of many Hardy Amies evening dresses worn by the Queen, when Princess Elizabeth, at the State Banquet at Rideau Hall, Ottawa, given by the Governor General on 10 October 1951 during the Royal Tour of Canada. The Princess is talking to Viscountess Alexander. The dress is of white lace threaded with gleaming gold tissue with the fashionable 'cracker' or fan neckline.*

Left: *Two Hardy Amies evening dress designs for the postponed tour of Australia and New Zealand in 1952. Above left: another crinoline design of tiered apricot-rose coloured lace frills both delivered in January 1952. Below left: the full skirt is given a starburst serpentine design to be later recreated in a similar dress worn for the State Visit to France in 1957.*

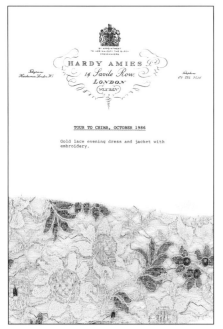

HARDY AMIES Ltd
14 Savile Row. W.1.
Telephone   Regent 0788

Evening dress in ice blue pure silk paper
taffeta, fitted bodice with full skirt.
Bodice and yoke of skirt trimmed silver
thread and diamanté embroidery.

Australia 1953/54

HARDY AMIES Ltd
14 Savile Row.
LONDON

TOUR TO CHINA, OCTOBER 1986

Gold lace evening dress and jacket with
embroidery.

Above: *An embroidered evening dress designed for warm Australian evenings. The dress was delivered in October 1953 ready to be included in the twelve tons of luggage accompanying the Royal Tour from November 1953 to May 1954.*

Left: *Three of the many samples of embroidery created over the decades by S. Lock & Company to accompany sketches submitted to the Queen by Hardy Amies for her approval. At the top is a sample for the kingfisher blue silk dress worn by Queen Elizabeth II for the final banquet held in the Louvre to conclude the State Visit to France 8th-11th April 1957. The serpentine effect of the band of embroidery began at the right shoulder of the dress and encircled the skirt of the dress, as seen on a dress designed in 1952 to be worn in Australia.*

Opposite page: *The design with an embroidered fabric sample of autumn leaves and berries for the evening dress worn at a dinner with President and Mrs Eisenhower, during the State Visit to the United States in October 1957. The stole in the design does not seem to have been used, if ordered.*

A.1.

AMIES *Ld*
ile Row. **W.1.** *Regent 0728.*

blue/gray heavy satin,
a design of autumn leaves
read and pearls. The wide
eated at the waist. The
hed with cuffs of plain
s the stole.

From 21 to 23 May 1957 the Queen paid a State Visit to Denmark. For an evening at the ballet she wore this Amies design of rich pearl and rhinestone embroidered apricot silk, the skirt with six deep folds. Amies suggested the colour as a foil to the pale blue ribbon of the Danish Order of the Elephant. A newspaper reported Amies commenting on the design: 'She did not hesitate for a minute'.

MARK 1957

Opposite page: The dress and its design, worn by the Queen at Government House Ottawa during her 1959 visit to Canada, and revealing the full bouffant fashionable outline of the time in the sketch. The multi-layered skirt with an embroidered voile top layer is gathered at the back with horizontal bands of ribbon, tied in the centre with bows.

Above: *The Hardy Amies House archive album embossed with 'The Queen' notes that this blue, black and white printed silk dress with a large floral design was the first time that such a print had been used for an evening dress. Worn here at a ballet performance during the second Commonwealth Heads of Government Meeting of July to August 1973.*

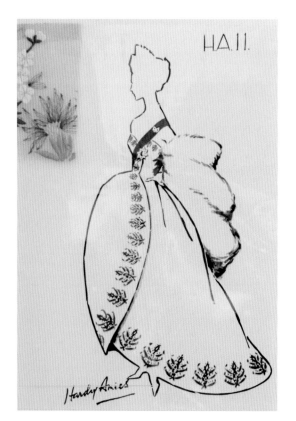

Above: *The design of the dress worn by the Queen during the State Visit to West Germany in 1965, the ribbon indicated is that of the Sonderstufe des Großkreuzes, only given by the Federal Republic of Germany to foreign heads of state and their spouses. (see full description page 162)*

Left: *One of several designs apparently submitted in 1959 and resulting in a similar dress which was worn by the Queen on 9 April 1960 at Covent Garden during the State Visit of General de Gaulle, and subsequently on 2 May 1960 at a Windsor Castle reception attended by Prime Minister Harold Macmillan and Commonwealth Prime Ministers.*

Opposite page: *Two Fleetwood-Amies designs for the Queen relating to the simple outline of mid-1960s design for evening dresses, the lower example worn during the Tour of Australia and New Zealand from March to May of 1970.*

No sleeves
Lower neckline
in front.

The Kenneth Fleetwood design for a dress worn by the Queen during the visit to the west coast of the United States on 3 March 1983. The dress attracted some adverse press criticism. Much to the designer's dismay, the topmost bows on the shoulders were later removed, but the Queen clearly liked the romantic design, and wore it during the State Visit to Sweden in May 1983, and again for three portraits by Mara McGregor. The portrait opposite hangs in the Parliament of New South Wales Building and depicts Queen Elizabeth II as Queen of Australia. (Reproduced by kind permission of the artist, and New South Wales Parliament Collection, Sydney.)

White organza evening dress with full soft white chiffon skirt and white organza bodice completely embroidered with Californian poppy motif.

Left: *Hardy Amies was present on the evening of 28 February 1983, when this dress was worn in Hollywood during the Queen's visit to the west coast of the United States. He deliberately chose to emulate Norman Hartnell's design idea in using an embroidered national flower on the Queen's dress as a tribute to the host nation, as with the Californian poppy seen here. The dress was later worn in 1985.*

Opposite page: *Norman Parkinson was commissioned to take a series of photographs of Queen Elizabeth the Queen Mother to commemorate her eightieth birthday in 1980. A short while before, he telephoned Hardy Amies on holiday to explain his idea for a less formal image of her with her daughters the Queen and Princess Margaret. Amies telephoned Jon Moore, who had the dark blue satin capes quickly made. Parkinson later wrote how Princess Margaret agreed to suggest the cape sitting to her mother and sister after the formal images had been taken. This was the only known occasion on which the Queen Mother wore anything made by Hardy Amies, and at the end of the session she reminded Amies not to forget his beautiful blue capes. He responded that the capes would never leave the Royal Lodge and that she might care to wear one for gardening. (Lifework, Norman Parkinson, photograph © Norman Parkinson Ltd/Courtesy Norman Parkinson Archive)*

Below: *A preliminary undated sketch for the design of a cape for the Queen. The Amies 1966 collections included twill cape-coats such as this.*

The rapport between the Queen and her designers extended to Amies, with some handwritten letters and exchanges of Christmas presents: for a few years Amies sent additions to the Queen's small menagerie of wooden animals. The letters also disprove press comments over the years, as they reveal the Queen's natural interest in new materials and patterns, the effect of climate conditions to be encountered in forthcoming visits

abroad, and a sense of economy in ordering what sometimes needed to be a large wardrobe which represented the best of Britain abroad. Many dresses or ensembles were subsequently worn more than once, a practice initiated at the beginning of her reign, and all her designers were used to executing alterations, repairs or changes to existing clothes, so that the life of the wardrobe might be usefully extended.

In 1989 Amies was created a Knight Commander of the Royal Victorian Order by the Queen. He said, 'When the letter came, I was alone, and I just sat down and burst into tears. It's a personal gift. Other people who get it are much more important than just a dressmaker.' (*Going Strong* p.18)

Hardy Amies summed up his view on the Queen's style, 'I consider the Queen chooses with impeccable taste and a wonderful sense of appropriateness, outfits which are always totally suitable for the occasion. It is [as] if the Queen knows her audience. I have never heard a criticism of the Queen's appearance from anyone present at a particular occasion.' (*SH* p.104) He then verbally laid into photographers and journalists, telling them they were overly critical of Her Majesty's appearance and always photographed her from an unflattering angle.

Chapter Eight

HARDY AMIES
AT HOME

Hardy Amies

Previous page: *Amies in the garden designed with Rosemary Verey and Alvilde Lees-Milne at his country house, The Old School, Langford, Oxfordshire, 1980.*

Above: *Leaders, Hodsoll Street, near Wrotham, Kent bought by Alexis and Anne ffrench in 1934 and transformed by him into a weekend retreat, circa 1935.*

Boys do not usually pester their parents to send them to boarding school, but Hardy Amies did. Life at home must have been uneasy, although he had fond memories of family holidays by the sea. His Brentwood English master Howard Hayden, reminiscing in 1979, said he was far more sophisticated and thoughtful than his contemporaries, 'His manners were exceptional, more from his own personality than his background, I suspect... He was like a thoroughbred among forest ponies.' Amies added, 'I always had to be well dressed. I made terrible scenes, if my mother couldn't manage... I wanted my first dinner suit at seventeen.' (*New Zealand Herald* 18 August 1979) His younger sister Rosemary spent a year in Germany, before returning to nurse her terminally-ill mother in 1937 and after her death in 1938, she looked after her father. He re-married in 1939, but the siblings did not adapt to their stepmother, also called Mary, and saw less of them after they moved to Deal and a family Christmas was abandoned.

From 1934 Hardy found complete domestic happiness with Anne and Alexis ffrench who lived in separate London flats, sharing weekends in the country. Both had children from previous marriages; Hardy became something of an older brother to them. Their isolated country cottage, curiously named 'Leaders', was completely remodelled by Alexis to include Kentish clapper-boarded facades, Neo-Regency Gothic windows and a slim-pillared porch. The large plot became a formal garden with antique architectural objects rescued from demolished houses, a speciality of his friend, the dealer Geoffrey Houghton-Brown.

The interior was changed and gained a comfortable drawing room with modern sofas, English and French antique furniture and elaborate curtains with swagged pelmets above French windows, opening onto to a paved terrace bordered by stone balustrades. The seventeenth-century dining room furniture stood on squares of rush matting, not often seen at that date, and the bedrooms reflected the Neo-Regency Gothic of the windows. John Fowler, a friend, visitor and admirer of the ffrench style, absorbed it into his own designs of interiors. The house appealed to many and was illustrated in magazines.

During the war, Leaders became a haven for many guests, not least for Amies, on leave from SOE. By 1946 twenty new council houses appeared opposite and French wrote, 'my weekends were consequently rendered hideous by barking mongrels, screaming children, and blaring radios… This time I was not going to be caught out and I bought my new house inside its own park.' (*Vogue* September 1948) On Saturday 4 January 1947 Amies noted 'Messing' in his diary and on Monday 7 April 'Goodbye to Leaders'.

Above: *Summer idyll for Amies, a constant weekend and wartime holiday visitor at Leaders, which is within easy commuting distance from London, circa 1939.*

Below: *The dining room at Leaders, where a welcome guest was their mutual friend John Fowler, who appreciated such 'humble elegance', using similar rush matting in his first London flat, circa 1935.*

Right: *In 1935 Alexis ffrench moved his recently established business from South Kensington to the Belgravia end of Pont Street, also taking and decorating the flat above. Amies in the hall, circa 1936.*

Below: *Alexis ffrench's Regency chinoiserie bedroom in Pont Street with canopied and frogged curtains, circa 1936.*

Messing Park has a Regency facade on a Queen Anne interior and is near both Kelvedon Hall, the Essex house of a friend, Sir Henry 'Chips' Channon, and Felix Hall lived in by Geoffrey Houghton-Brown. He probably suggested it to ffrench, just as he had 14 Savile Row to Amies. Mr and Mrs ffrench continued their living arrangements, and Alexis' daughter Jackie acted as *chatelaine* at Messing in their absence. Alexis and Hardy had suites of their own, and were looked after by a small staff, including young Vincenzina, who had recently come to join her brother in England from Italy to work in the Tiptree jam factory. She was interviewed by Mrs ffrench and delighted to leave the factory for the glamorous surroundings of Messing, where she was soon adopted as a member of the family, playing with Jackie's small son Michael and apart from her domestic duties, also cleaned silver and antiques for Alexis ffrench's London business. She later moved to Alexis and Hardy's shared London house and the final ffrench country house in Kent.

At Messing, sophisticated interiors relied on coupon-free materials: dyed dust cloth for curtains and felt for the floors, overlaid with beautiful antique

A contemporary watercolour of the Pont Street Neo-Regency drawing room, circa 1938 (below) and a photograph of the same view, circa 1938 (left).

carpets. The grey and white painted Gothic library and Bamboo Room with elephant and pink walls represent a new post-war grand manner, adopted by many decorators including Fowler, and were redolent of the last interiors by Syrie Maugham, another guest. Messing was sold in 1955 and a substitute found in Malmains Manor, Alkham, a sixteenth-century house with nineteenth-century facades, behind the white cliffs of Dover.

In 1934 Amies had wearied of commuting from Becontree to Lachasse. He met friends such as John Fowler for lunch at The Running Footman, near Lachasse, but usually had to curtail his evenings to catch the last train home. ffrench provided a solution in his new flat at 42 Pont Street, offering Amies a room in return for supervision of the staff and supplies; Amies' bank book records him paying his way by monthly cheques.

The Pont Street arrangement was dissolved in early 1940, and by 1941 a nearby flat at 14 Chesham Place was found, furnished by ffrench, and used until they moved to 22 Eldon Road, Kensington in 1953. By then ffrench was very unwell, but managed a last Italian holiday with Anne and

Hardy Amies at Home

Moving times: top 'I'm mad about the Jensen, you're lined up at the lights, and you're away, whoosh, like that!' Ian Fleming had the right idea about cars. His had to be tough enough to stand outside, yet be able to start up immediately.' Hardy had the interior re-designed. There were nine different colours and textures, all replaced by tan leather and the dashboard stripped of chrome and a sun roof fitted. The central arm rest contained a pair of hair brushes. This navy blue car carried his number plate EHA 1, formerly on his Rover. Seen outside 14 Savile Row, 1966; middle: Alexis ffrench and Hardy in the Humber Super Snipe returning to London after a weekend at Malmains, Alkham, Kent. They are seen off by Vincenzina, who had previously worked at Messing Park, Essex, 1954; bottom: Folly, one of Hardy's first dachshunds, perched in front of the radiator of the ffrench Rolls-Royce, 1950.

Hardy, eventually succumbing to cancer of the bone marrow and amputation of a leg. Anne was with him at Malmains, whilst Hardy accompanied him to numerous doctors in London. After Alexis' death, Hardy still visited Malmains and had visitors, entertaining his father from nearby Deal. This was the second time that Hardy had witnessed the painful death from cancer of someone he loved, and he was fated to relive it twice more with Ken Fleetwood and Rosemary.

22 Eldon Road was run impeccably by Vincenzina and her husband Barrie. Amies now buried himself in his career, and by 1965 the house was too small for entertaining on a large scale. After a temporary stay at number 26 (from 12 December 1965 to 25 March 1966) he moved into the larger house at 17b which was his London home from 25 March 1966 until 9 July 1980. The visitors' books contain the signatures of members of the Royal Family, aristocrats of all nations, world-famous stars of the opera, ballet, stage, screen and literary worlds, in fact, anyone well known for some achievement in late twentieth-century life, all mixed with other friends and business associates. Vincenzina particularly remembered Princess Margaret, Loelia, Duchess of Westminster and Vivien Leigh. In 1980 he moved to a more compact ground floor flat in nearby Cornwall Gardens.

By then, Amies was established in Langford, which struck Sir Roy Strong as 'one of those dream Cotswold villages where no peasants exist and everyone has a large bank balance and lives in a rose-embowered stone house or cottage.' Amies had given Rosemary the money to buy herself a flat, after she ceased working at Hardy Amies Ltd at Savile Row. He was

surprised and pleased that, not liking London life, she found Bakery Cottage, Langford and renovated it, settling in with an old friend from WVS days, Gwyn Owen. Both lived there until the end of their lives. Once again Hardy was impressed by his sister's common sense, and in 1972 he bought, rebuilt and extended the old schoolhouse in the same village, so possessing his only country house, where he gave generous hospitality to a variety of people – not all grand – for the rest of his life, as he did in London.

For the interiors, he used early 'brown furniture', going against the taste of ffrench and Fowler, to create his own style based on a love of seventeenth-century history and architectural design. Austere stone and plain wood

Above: 'Amies gave the strangest party since the first night of Auntie Mame was given in a Turkish bath.' For Hardy's first Ice Party, Kenneth Alexander Partridge designed a fantasy with frosted trees, waiters on skates and sleighs for the less active. Guests included the Duchesses of Bedford and Devonshire, the Marchioness of Dufferin and Ava, Lady Lewisham, Vivien Leigh, Edith Evans, Lady Pamela Berry and George Weidenfeld. 20 November 1958.

Right, top: Hardy Amies accompanies the then Lady Harewood at the opening of Leeds Rank Ice Rink in 1962. An Amies client, she also opened that year's London Fashion Week wearing an Amies dress and coat.

Right, below: A non-athlete at school, Amies first played tennis in Solihull at weekends away from his work with Avery Scales in Birmingham during the early 1930s and continued during the war. He subsequently combined designing fortnights in Torquay with professional lessons, seen here circa 1958, maintained until in his eighties.

Right: *From 1953 Amies shared 22 Eldon Road, Kensington with Alexis ffrench until his death in 1956, remaining until 1966. The drawing room interiors reflect ffrench's sophisticated blending of French and English styles, the Warner Fabrics silk curtains came from a 1946 bale of silk too heavy for Amies' evening dresses*

Below: *The basement dining room contained a marble-topped dining table, which Amies came to dislike as cold and noise inducing, circa 1956.*

were used, softened by tapestry, not least his needlepoint. Ingeniously fitted bathrooms and a large kitchen added to the comfort. There is a German feel to the newer interiors, stronger than a resemblance to earlier English buildings, such as the Cambridge colleges Amies always regretted not being part of in his youth. Amies paid £4000 for his house and £40,000 on the works.

Whilst he still had his Italian cook Rina in London, he would arrive in Langford with bags of delicious prepared casseroles, pâtés and fish pies, 'I'm meals on wheels', he would say. Supplies exhausted, he would attend to simple cooking himself. Two dachshunds would greet him, having left the London pair at home, and seasonal log fires with bowls of lavender from the garden scented the air.

The Amies garden was a clever plan by Rosemary Verey acting on instructions to keep the area as low-maintenance as possible, 'There was never any question of there being any grass' he wrote. He also sought a remembrance of the past in his garden, 'I loved roses when I was eight. There was a climbing 'Richmond' on the wall of my parents' tiny garden... I couldn't find one and had to be content with climbing 'Crimson Glory'.' He summed up the overall design, 'I also like symmetry. I suppose it is impossible to be a dress designer and not admire the proportions of the human body. I do indeed, and symmetry and balance contribute much to its beauty. There are pairs of several things: ears, eyes, arms, bosoms and gentlemen's things which we can't talk about. And where there is anything single, like a nose, a navel or anything still less mentionable, these are bang in the middle. So it has to be with my garden. The site was very irregular. I ignored this and made my plans in accordance with the alignment of the French windows in my new dining room. I set the axis of the garden and tool care to have equally sized beds on either side of the path. The focal point of this is the summerhouse, I need to provide shade on a summer's day, for the stone paths and terraces are sometimes too hot.' (*The Englishman's Garden*, p.16) In the summer-house is a plaque incised with a Latin dedication penned by his old friend from SOE days, the politician Enoch Powell.

From 1966 until 1980 Amies lived in the larger 17b Eldon Road, designed with Michael Raymond of Colefax & Fowler. The Victorian interiors were renovated and re-modelled as spacious rooms for entertaining, circa 1968.

Hardy Amies at Home

Right: *The drawing room absorbed furniture from his previous house at number 22 Eldon Road, augmented by modern lighting, ruched curtains, white pile carpets and sleek new leather sofas, circa 1968.*

Left, top: *Hardy Amies living with the height of 1960s sophisticated interior design, in front of the dominant painting in the drawing room by Graham Sutherland, circa 1968.*

Left, bottom: *During the 1960s, the Amies brand became famous in the United States. Hardy Amies became a favourite guest of many socialites in America at parties similar to this, given by a devoted friend and client, Maureen, Lady Dudley (1932-2011). Born Maureen Swanson, she became a minor 1950s British film star, and retired from acting in 1961 on her marriage to Viscount Ednam, who succeeded as Earl of Dudley in 1969. Lady Dudley is seen here wearing an Amies dress.*

Opposite page: *The walled school yard at Langford, unused since 1934, became an easily maintained garden in the 1970s. By the time of this picture, circa 1980, the planting had matured.*

The old schoolroom transformed by Colefax & Fowler with a splendid Jacobean chimney-piece with strap-work carving and a portrait of Catherine of Braganza hanging above; doors to the far left lead to the kitchen. At the end of his life Amies impressed Sir Roy Strong as 'a country gent in rookery nook Jacobean making his exit via the parish church'. (Author correspondence, June 2012)

'The Winter Queen', Elizabeth Stuart, Queen of Bohemia (reigned 4 November 1619 - 8 November 1620) was the daughter of James I and Anne of Denmark. Hardy Amies was enthralled with the life of 'The Winter Queen', not least because of her relationship to the current British Royal Family. Elizabeth's youngest daughter Sophia married Ernst Augustus, who became Elector of Hanover in 1658. Sophia became the Protestant heir to the crowns of England and Ireland and by The Act of Settlement, the succession was settled on Sophia and her issue. All monarchs of Great Britain succeeding George I are therefore descendants of Elizabeth. Amies bought this portrait in 1989.

Later, he lived more at Langford. The sage-like aspect of his nature, noted by Ian Garlant, led to tart exchanges with friends, as Sir Roy Strong witnessed. Amies referred to '…the Laskett garden as "Mr Pooter goes to Versailles". My wife was ticked off for decking her recreation of a room in the diarist Samuel Pepys' house in an exhibition at the National Portrait Gallery with dried hydrangeas. "They didn't arrive before the eighteenth century" was the withering putdown, to which Julia replied, "Well they should have done as they look right." ' (author correspondence with RS, 2012) Amies had a passion for auriculas, and early tulips (after a reprimand by Fowler on the colour he had chosen) and formed a large horticultural library.

Roy Strong was also subjected to Amies' recurring thoughts on The Winter Queen, 'For some weird reason he had a passion for James I's daughter Elizabeth, Queen of Bohemia, The Winter Queen. He even embroidered seat covers with patterns from the knots in her garden at Heidelberg…' Selina Hastings, a good friend, considers this a reflection of his admiration for strong women. (author conversation with SH, 2012) Another friend, Derek Granger, said that Fleetwood was best at checking the 'Winter Queen' flow, 'Oh, he's off again, why can't he give it a rest?'

The drawing room looking to the hall, the dining room door on the far right. Needlework on the chairs and cushions by Amies, circa 1980.

Hardy Amies at Home

Right: *Two oak seventeenth-century chairs with needlepoint cushions, circa 1990. Hardy worked during flights around the world or in quiet moments from the 1950s onwards.*

Below: *The Hardy Amies book-plate with references to Sheridan, dressmaking, design and gardens, an early example of the work of Martin Battersby (1914-82), the acclaimed trompe l'oeil painter, muralist and historian of twentieth-century decorative arts. The Latin motto was invented with Yvonne ffrench and translates as 'Less Than Art: Greater Than Trade'. The book to the left from Amies' or Battersby's collection, La Belle Assemblée, was 'Bell's Court and Fashionable Magazine Addressed Particularly to the Ladies', a British illustrated journal published from 1806 to 1837. Hardy spent considerable sums at the book dealers Heywood Hill during and after the war and he may well have bought a copy there. From an early age, Amies was an avid book collector, amassing a large library in four languages especially on the history of fashion and French literature. Balzac was a particular favourite.*

He had early on in his friendship with them, adopted the ffrench family interests and also John Fowler's own fascination with Marie Antoinette, nurturing his own specialist subject based, he said, on an interest in the Stuarts and the origins of the Royal Family. Early on Anne ffrench had said, 'Understand the Plantagenets and you have the whole key.' Hardy, Rosemary and their friends Mr and Mrs Max Ulfane, owners of Ashdown House near Langford, later embarked on a full tour of the European sites relating to the The Winter Queen.

He also had literary passions, begun at an early age. He read E.F. Benson's novels at the age of nine in the train on the way to school. He particularly liked the novels of Balzac, which were to be found in several editions amongst his books and which he liked to read peacefully in bed. A small illustrated book on the Flemish artist Ensor was published in Brussels in 1944 and marks the termination of his SOE career there. Many books were presented by friends, often marking events and associations, such as the leather-bound 1825 *Memoirs of the Life of Sheridan* bearing the Middleton Park bookplate of the Earl of Jersey and his own, clearly a present from Lady Jersey, Virginia Cherrill, commemorating their friendship and business association, when he opened at 14 Savile Row. An illustrated work on the eighteenth-century French court architect Ledoux given to *'Cher Hardy en souvenir d'un après midi en printemps'* is signed by Michel de Brunhoff, the celebrated editor of French *Vogue* related to Nina Leclercq, who had left French *Vogue* to set up the Amies Boutique. Hardy had needlessly worried that de Brunhoff would be upset.

Opposite page: *Always enthusiastic and professional in what he did, Amies became proficient in needlepoint, often undertaken on long flights. On one he sat next to an Australian acquaintance and ignored all attempts to make conversation. The man took out his own petit-point, later reporting that Hardy's was more gros-point than his own petit-point. His needlepoint carpet would eventually be used to cover his coffin. (© Norman Parkinson Ltd/Courtesy Norman Parkinson Archive, circa 1989)*

Right: *Amies bought and converted an old barn to house Langford guests, audio equipment and an expanding collection of music recordings. It also doubled as a pavilion for the tennis court laid outside. The dining room had tiles from the Amies ranges of the 1970s.*

Below: *Part hunting lodge, part English stage-set drawing room, the barn was looked after by a small staff, supervised by his sister Rosemary, who had been the first to move to the village.*

A passionate lover of music and constant visitor to Covent Garden, Glyndebourne and Salzburg, Amies was well-versed in opera lore, but not an opera bore. In September 1958 he was the guest on the BBC radio programme *Desert Island Discs*, choosing as his eight records Wagner's Overture to 'Die Meistersinger', Debussy's 'Letter Song' sung by Clare Croiza, Beethoven's 'Archduke' piano trio, Mozart's 'Il mio tesoro' sung by Richard Tauber, Puccini's 'Humming Chorus' from *Madame Butterfly*, Bach's Brandenburg Concerto No 3, Verdi's 'Ella giammai m'amò' from *Don Carlos* and, Richard Strauss's 'Ist ein Traum' (Act 3 Duet Finale) from *Der Rosenkavalier*. The audio equipment at Langford and recordings were superb and Amies studied the scores and libretti of operas. He was also friends with Joan Sutherland, a good client, and through Alexis ffrench had become a friend of the soprano Olga Lynn. During the war, he had made friends with David Webster, later Director General at Covent Garden and was invited to attend rehearsals, including those for *Gloriana*, meeting the composer Benjamin Britten, and also attending the Royal Gala performance and premiere in honour of the Queen's Coronation in 1953. Music was a passion. Incidentally, his luxury item chosen for the desert island was a dressing case!

Rosemary was also capable of holding her own against Hardy's often extreme attitudes; talking about the new London house 17b Eldon Road, she said, 'I get busy with the Black and Decker, whilst he lies there reading *Vogue*.' Rosemary found the local craftsmen for the works on Hardy's Langford house, chose the blue-grey brick floors and even had the old Taynton quarry stone reused for the building work. It was formerly used for St. Pauls Cathedral, Windsor Castle and many Oxford buildings.

Fleetwood sometimes teased Rosemary about her lack of imagination and ingrained attitudes, 'we have a new resident coming to the village... an Oxford professor of anthropology... yes, he even has tribal markings, but his face is so dark they don't really show.' (Derek Granger ob. cit) She was totally loyal to Hardy, as proved by a 1991 interview,' What makes me cross is when journalists ask my brother stupid questions about dress-designing and the Queen and make out he's some sort of effeminate creature. He isn't. He's a linguist, a historian and an operaphile. Hardy gives me dresses. He's always trying to alter my basic look, but he shan't succeed. He says: "Wear this" and I say: "No... don't like it." I remember him saying "My favourite customers are the rich". Now that's a facetious Hardy remark. I don't like the word snob, but Hardy hasn't got the ability to talk to everyone like I have. I don't mind if they're very common.' (undated newspaper article) Nevertheless, life in the Amies households was no more than mildly eccentric, even if Hardy Amies tended to become more outspoken with age.

'His final putdown in my case', wrote Sir Roy Strong 'was at a dinner given at the Garrick Club in honour of the gardener Rosemary Verey's (1918-2001) eightieth birthday. I went to greet Hardy saying that I was busy arranging

Hardy and Rosemary. Always close to his younger sister, she became his rock after the death of Ken Fleetwood. He was devastated when she also died before him.

215

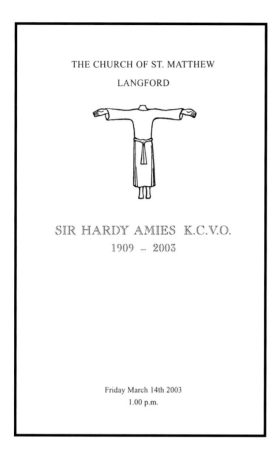

THE CHURCH OF ST. MATTHEW
LANGFORD

SIR HARDY AMIES K.C.V.O.
1909 – 2003

Friday March 14th 2003
1.00 p.m.

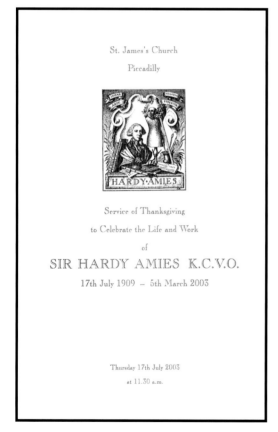

St. James's Church
Piccadilly

Service of Thanksgiving
to Celebrate the Life and Work
of
SIR HARDY AMIES K.C.V.O.
17th July 1909 – 5th March 2003

Thursday 17th July 2003
at 11.30 a.m.

The Orders of Service for the burial and memorial services of Sir Hardy Amies KCVO.

the "placement" to which came the stentorian reply, "Dear boy, never use that expression. It's the word the French use for what they do with their money. The correct term is *place a table*". Towards the end of his life, Hardy had another pre-occupation with "Handbag Money". 'I always want more of it. Have you got enough?' (author conversation with HA) What would Lady Bracknell have made of that?

Hardy Amies was given an eightieth birthday party at nearby Buscot Park by his friends, the owners Lord and Lady Faringdon. Amongst the guests were Selina Hastings who went with mutual friends Alvilde and James Lees-Milne, who recorded the event with a mixture of envy, condescension and horror in his diary of Monday, 17 July 1989: 'posh surroundings and gold plate'. He was seated between the Duchess of Devonshire on Hardy's left, and Lady Lindsay (formerly Loelia, Duchess of Westminster). 'At one point I took my napkin and wiped food off her chin'. Other guests included 'Princess Peg' (Margaret, Princess of Hesse) on Hardy's right, Lords Bathurst and Briggs and other figures from Hardy's past, such as Peter Coats 'a white skeleton'. Hardy's speech was 'well-delivered but embarrassing' as it referred to his humble 'corrected to humdrum' origins and went on to thank various guests for their 'patronage' and for his welcome at Chatsworth. 'Call me snobbish, but I thought all this rather ill-bred. A pity for he is a dear man… Is to be knighted this week.' Ian Garlant provides another vignette of the evening, 'It was an entirely private party to which a journalist had somehow gained access…he was unexpectedly confronted by the question: 'What do you think is your greatest achievement?' 'Hardy Amies of course', was the irritated reply. 'Do you mean the House or the Company?' asked the journalist. 'Neither you idiot… I mean ME!' (Introduction to 2007 edition of *ABC of Men's Fashion*) Three months later on Wednesday, 31 October 1990 Lees-Milne noted Hardy and Tom Parr as ushers at Peter Coats' memorial service in London. Hardy's generation of wartime survivors was beginning to die off.

By not letting go of his life at Hardy Amies Ltd until the bitter end, he perpetuated his reputation, led a scaled-down yet comfortable lifestyle, and had a strong impetus to keep going. Ian Garlant first met him aged seventy-seven. 'The overwhelming impression he gave was of an inquisitive, still enthusiastic man, engaged in observing the world around him; there was nothing old about him.' *(Op cit)* The decline was inevitable, but managed with great style until the end with the help of David Freeman, who had also cared for Rosemary.

The final Hardy Amies Show is recorded by Sir Roy Strong in his autobiography. 'David Freeman had organised everything perfectly. The coffin was draped with the carpet Hardy had worked with all his favourite flowers acting as a hearse cloth. On top of it was placed his KCVO and swathes of more favourite flowers. Inside had been tucked a sprig of rosemary from his own garden and, at the last minute, a sprig was

plucked from his sister Rosemary's garden to join the other flowers. The church was very near and I brought up the rear of the procession. Inside it was crammed and outside there was a sprinkling of press photographers which would have pleased him. Hardy epitomised the standards of a vanished generation, one which believed in hard work, exact attention to detail and the observation of the niceties of social life. He was the epitome of a certain type of Englishness whose essence was restraint mingled with splendour. He was a stickler for what he considered correct dress.' Sir Roy Strong's words prove a fitting epitaph, 'When he died a bit of Old England went'.

Above: A lunch party in the Old School, Langford. Hardy stands to toast the photographer with Kenneth Fleetwood in the foreground, and Rosemary seated left with their mutual friend David Freeman, Hardy's heir. He was curator of Tredegar House, Monmouthshire from 1979-97 and a mutual friend; the architectural historian James Lees-Milne, considered that he made a 'signal success' in his work there. Befriended by Rosemary, Freeman became an indispensible part of the Hardy Amies household after her death. More recently, he has worked as consultant curator at Buscot Park, Oxfordshire, the country house of Lord and Lady Faringdon.

Right: The letter sent by Hardy Amies to those congratulating him on his knighthood and the insignia of the Knight Commander of the Royal Victorian Order, within the personal gift of the Queen and recognising his service.

14, SAVILE ROW, W1X 2JN

01-734 2436

I was, of course, delighted to be given such a high ranking and personal award from the Queen.

Equally touching is the kindness of friends who have sent me such charming letters.

Please accept my deep gratitude.

Chapter Nine

Hardy Amies
The Merchant

Hardy Amies

Hardy Amies the Merchant

Previous page: Hardy Amies opened his in-house Boutique in July 1950 and a celebratory party followed on the birthday of HM King George VI, 14 December 1950. The Boutique offered increasingly sophisticated luxuries, such as scent which was launched in 1958.

For roughly four years before the outbreak of war in 1939, London had become a fashion centre beginning to rival Paris, increasingly of interest to the economically important North American store buyers and private clients. Some Parisian Houses responded by opening London branches amongst the growing number of successful young British designers, led by the founder of this new fashion movement, Norman Hartnell, who capitalised on his fame by creating three scents. Amies was a sponge to such commercial activity.

At Lachasse, Amies not only established a rapport with store buyers, but also mass-producers of women's clothing; his innovations in women's suit construction were successfully adapted by many manufacturers. After the war Amies determined that he would benefit financially from the mass-production and marketing he had observed being applied to his own wartime designs of Utility clothing. Soon after opening his own House in 1946, he had to rethink his strategy, as in February 1947, Dior's 'New Look' made all designers' creations appear démodé overnight – even more so in London, where Austerity measures and clothes rationing were still firmly in place. Although there was much resistance to the extravagant new fashion and even street demonstrations in America, Amies recognised that if London were to remain a viable fashion centre, couture design would have to adapt the radical Parisian lead into something uniquely British. He noted that Chanel had been a good client of British mills – Amies also relied upon their superlative cloth for his export collections of coats and suits: North American buyers loved them. He also liked to quote Chanel, for once not sarcastically, 'La mode a deux buts: le confort et l'amour. La beaute c'est quand elle y arrive.' (*JSF* p.175)

KENDALS IS _YOUR_ STORE

Hardy Amies' Boutique presents a Black and White novelty striped worsted suit of impeccable tailoring. Buttoned revers edged with pique, and a velvet collar on the jacket. The front of the skirt is elegantly slim with neat pleating at the back.

Hardy Amies' Boutique suit of fine worsted repp. Soft rounded shoulder line, moulded hip line, high fastening jacket. Arrow slim skirt has three deep pleats at the back.
Hardy Amies' Boutique of Ready-to-wear Suits and Coats—Second Floor.

Suits by Hardy Amies Boutique

KENDAL MILNE & C? MANCHESTER 3.

The Boutique was conceived as a less expensive source of Hardy Amies clothes, housed in a showroom at the back of the ground floor. Ready-to-wear suits and coats were given separate shows, first to the press and then to retail outlets. A separate company was set up from 50 Grosvenor Street, conceived with manufacturer Alex Brenner with suits made by his brother Simon, respected for the quality of their mass-produced garments made with the latest machinery. The Amies label was bought by many large independent department stores within the British Isles and North America, such as Kendals (above) and B. Altman (left).

Hardy Amies the Merchant

In spring 1950, Amies visited his old friend Nina Leclercq, Fashion Editor with French Vogue in Paris. They explored the existing boutiques of such couturiers as Marcel Rochas, Schiaparelli and Christian Dior, where Amies had an instructive full tour behind the scenes. Amies offered her a directorship of his company, and was amazed and delighted when she accepted his offer, Miss Leclercq became a powerful figure in the development of the Hardy Amies Boutique. In 1983 she dedicated a new copy of The Man Who Was Vogue *to Hardy, 'Dearest Hardy, Souvenir of Place du Palais Bourbon 1950' (a reference to her flat in Paris and their planning of the Boutique). The Boutique invoice highlights one satisfied customer!*

Amies was utterly pragmatic. He realised that Paris would continue to dominate world fashion, not least because of Dior, 'The New Look had many virtues. It not only returned women to the bondage of long skirts; it has kept manufacturers on their toes ever since. They are frightened lest another New Look should creep up on them unawares. If the New Look had gone blithely on its way, fashionable women would be thinking of wearing some sort of modified crinoline on the streets. I think I have seen Dior seen somewhere described as having a grandmother complex... I should like a humble little niche beside him in this respect.' (*JSF* p.174)

With the establishment of the Hardy Amies Boutique, he entered the ready-to-wear market and by early 1952 noted a newspaper headline, 'The Top Ten & The Great Fashion World Illusion... the 'rag trade' has £1,000,000 of sales a day. If the Top Ten [members of INCSOC] vanished, trade would go on... they sell on price and look, all copying one another and the designers. The only time they were caught out was with the New Look.' (*Sunday Chronicle* 3 February 1952) Hardy Amies had a workforce of less than one half of a Parisian couture House. He needed to produce about two thousand couture garments a year to create a reasonable profit and found great difficulty in finding the work-force capable of doing so in London. His co-members of INCSOC all had the same problems, of which the most acute was a lack of capital. Wages and rents were still at a reasonable pre-war level, from Amies' point of view, but were already beginning their inexorable rise. In 1954 Amies wrote about his workforce, '... I am a conductor of an orchestra, or let us muddle our similes completely, I am the father of a family. Indeed, this paternal aspect of the affair I look on most seriously as the years go by.' (*JSF* p.166) In 1952 Stanley Cox, who had trained with Molyneux, wrote out in his meticulous small script the details of staffing since 1946. It is worth reading them to realise that the running of Hardy Amies was no easy matter financially:

Showroom	Office	5 Beginners	1 Packer
4 Saleswomen	Secretary	*Eileen*	1 Fitter
4 Assistants	2 Ledger Clerks	3 Skirthands	1 Tailor
4 Models	1 Junior Clerk	3 Assistants	1 Tailoress
2 junior Assistants	1 Wages Clerk	*Odette*	3 Dresmakers
1 receptionist	1 Costing Clerk	1 second	3 Assistants
	1 Switchboard op.	12 Gownhands	1 Accountant
Stockroom		13 Assistants	1 Clerk
Stock Keeper	**Workrooms**	5 Beginners	
2 Indoor Assistants	*Leonard*	[*Miss*] *Beard*	**Porters, cleaning,**
2 Outdoor Assistants	1 second	1 Second	**maintenance**
(matchers)	5 Tailors	8 Gownhands	1 Caretaker Boilerman
	16 Tailoresses	10 Assistants	1 Doorman
	3 Improvers (men & Boys)	3 Beginners	1 maintenance man
Despatch	17 Assistants		1 Chauffeur
1 Packer	3 Beginners		6 part-time cleaners (6-9am)
1 Driver	*Ernest*	**Boutique**	
	1 second	*Miss Leclercq*	
Studio	3 Tailors	1 Assistant	**Canteen**
2 Artists	13 Tailoresses	1 Secretary	Cook Supervisor
1 Secretary	3 Improvers	2 Saleswomen	1 Assistant
	11 Assistants	1 Model	1 Kitchen hand
		3 Assistants	1 canteen assistant

Woman

Special Pattern

THIS DRESS BY

HARDY AMIES

SEE INSIDE

The Queen's Personal Friends

COMPLETE STORY

THE KISS OF
NORA WILSON

Hardy Amies signed a contract with the mass-circulation magazine Woman, *just as the Boutique and royal commissions were making the headlines. In the pre-television age, women everywhere received lifestyle news, views and visual inspiration from a variety of such magazines with circulation figures far outstripping those of* Vogue, *which remains the ultimate in fashion reporting. (*Woman *magazine archive/IPC Syndication)*

Right: *Amies was not alone amongst British couturiers in lending his name to a variety of promotional editorial features in the press, and here sums up the look of the period with a make-up specialist, at a time when British women were famous abroad for their lavish use of cosmetics, especially powder. Circa 1956.*

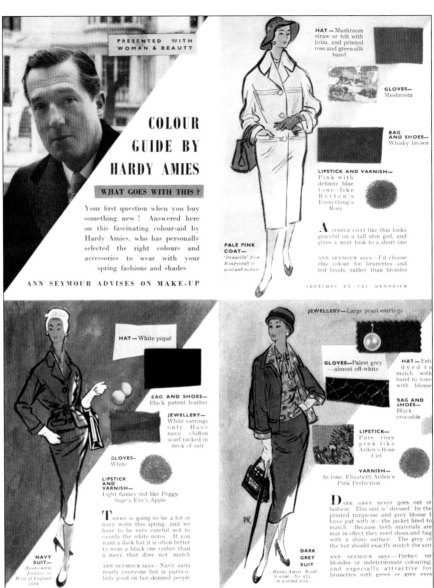

Left: *It was unusual for famous men to personally endorse such products in 1950s Britain, but the clever wording says it all. Martini, Cinzano and other exotic-sounding alcoholic drinks from the Continent became increasingly widespread as fashionable cocktail party ingredients. The connection made here between the product and 'a man with a reputation for understanding the good things in life' was a mutually profitable association. Amies, known to his friends as a good cook, was also seen in promotions for Constance Spry, who ran a school for florists and cookery, and had catered at Westminster for those attending the Coronation.*

Opposite page: *Hardy Amies received valuable free publicity by endorsing the latest man-made materials used in his collections, as with this draped and tied spotted jersey dress made from one of the many experimental yarns of the era. The Mondrian-inspired studio set reflects the latest in early 1950s decoration. Circa 1954.*

Hardy Amies

uses the beautiful
'Celanese' jersey
to mould this dress
of curving grace.
Such suppleness of
texture is inherent
in fabrics made from

'Celanese'
ACETATE YARN

Above: 'Hardy Perennial', as the fashion press now often termed him, approaching his seventieth birthday at home in his New York apartment on the twenty-fourth floor. In the early 1980s it was re-decorated with the aid of Imogen Taylor of Colefax & Fowler in the 'English' style of the period. Amies maintained that it was impossible to understand modern art without visiting the city.

Left: The New York apartment formed a useful springboard for visits to the Far East, Australia and New Zealand by Amies and the merchandising director Roger Whiteman, later sometimes joined by Kenneth Fleetwood.

Opposite page: Hardy Amies' Anglo-American alliance was given a boost by his high-profile connection with General Motors Cadillac division. Here, two romantic evening-dresses are photographed against the world-famous setting of the Victoria Memorial in front of Buckingham Palace. The styling of the Cadillac, a 1950s symbol of post-war American prosperity, blends with the confidence of Amies' own designs. Such cars could easily accommodate the full skirts of the dresses and bear their wearer to country clubs from Maine to Florida, first night theatre trips in New York or The Oscars in Hollywood. Amies relished the American dream from his earliest post-war visits and in the 1960s often participated in it.

It would be difficult to imagine a more wonderful place for a lady to sit than in the passenger seat of a new 1957 Cadillac. To begin with, she is marvelously comfortable. The seat cushions are soft and restful . . . the car's interior is wonderfully spacious . . . and every imaginable motoring convenience is close at hand. And how regal she feels! For she is literally surrounded by beauty and luxury and elegance. Why not stop in soon—with the man in your life—and spend an hour in the new "car of cars"? It's an experience you owe to yourself—and your dealer will be happy to accommodate you at any time.

CADILLAC MOTOR CAR DIVISION • GENERAL MOTORS CORPORATION

Cadillac

Gowns by Hardy Amies, photographed at Buckingham Palace expressly for Cadillac

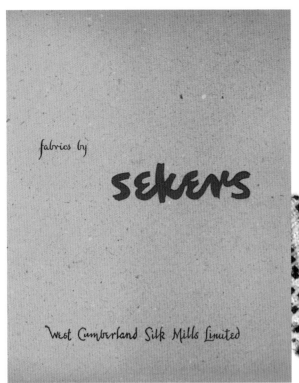

Above: *A Sekers promotional booklet, with a sample of 'Goodwood' a black and grey silk textile with a herringbone pattern. It was used by Hardy Amies for a town and country suit, Spring 1952. The Hardy Amies page was amongst those devoted to other distinguished clients such as Jacques Fath and Christian Dior. Most couturiers in England and France used Sekers' original materials. Amies was a friend of the co-founder and owner Miki Sekers, both sharing a love of Glyndebourne opera.*

Below: *Another piece of Sekers-Amies publicity in the form of a celebratory cake for Amies, presented with full press coverage and proving that both could have their cake and eat it.*

This workforce totalled two hundred and twelve, a fraction of those employed by Dior, enviably backed by the textile manufacturer Marcel Boussac and promoted with the assistance of the French government. In his first autobiography *Just So Far*, Amies devotes several chapters to the way in which all these people worked for him: it was an expensive business.

During his productive 1950 spring break in Paris with Nina Leclercq they visited Dior's House, from top to bottom, as well as other Houses to see what money-spinning innovations they might copy. Out of this visit and subsequent discussions, the Hardy Amies Boutique was born. 'The *Boutiques* were departments within the great French dress Houses and their style and method of working varied greatly from House to House. Marcel Rochas, for instance, had a *Boutique* of frivolities where fanciful gloves, jewellery, parasols and other little fantasies are sold side by side with his famous scents. Schiaparelli, on the other hand, laid more emphasis on selling ready-to-wear sports clothes, not letting amusing designs interfere with their practical use: whereas Dior would have in his Boutique an important collection of clothes which would be made to measure, with perhaps only one fitting, and being of simpler construction than those in the big collection upstairs, would be considerably cheaper. All these schemes were, of course, designed to bridge the gap between the swelling prices of made-to-measure *couture* clothes and the shrinking incomes of the regular customers.'(*JSF* p.160)

Right, top: *From early on Amies associated his name with Rayne, leading 'Shoemakers by Appointment', often using Rayne shoes for in-house models. He designed this shoe for Rayne in mid-1956. Managing director Edward Rayne became well-known from the 1950s and was adept at using innovative designers for shoes and the Bond Street shop was re-modelled with 1950s neo-Regency verve by Oliver Messel.*

Right, centre and bottom: *By 1970 the Amies name was used on an expanding range of products including men's shoe designs, here typifying the taste for fashionable wide-toed casual styles.*

Below: *Labels. By the mid-1960s the Hardy Amies label was not only attached to couture garments (top), but also to an increasing range of women's and menswear.*

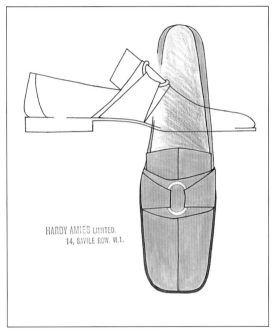

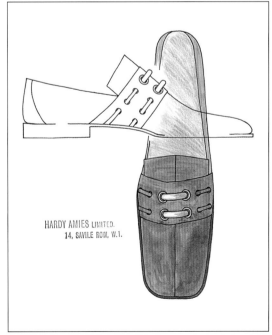

Above and left: *With the rapid success of Amies menswear, a variety of accessories were added to the ties (designed and sold under the Amies name from the late 1950s), including hats and gloves.*

The touch
of fur

Center vent, slit palm kid-skin gloves, by Hardy Amies, are silk lined. $14 at Bergdorf-Goodman.

Opposite: *American men noticed the Amies name on his* Esquire *magazine columns and 1964 book* ABC of Men's Fashion, *adding to forceful advertising campaigns and personal appearances in the USA by Amies, capitalising on two decades of sales visits. By 1969 he had a New York apartment and was a celebrity.*

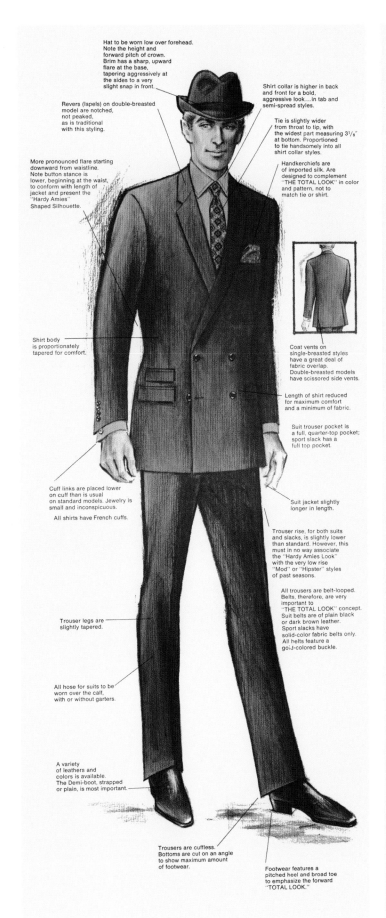

Hat to be worn low over forehead. Note the height and forward pitch of crown. Brim has a sharp, upward flare at the base, tapering aggressively at the sides to a very slight snap in front.

Revers (lapels) on double-breasted model are notched, not peaked, as is traditional with this styling.

More pronounced flare starting downward from waistline. Note button stance is lower, beginning at the waist, to conform with length of jacket and present the "Hardy Amies" Shaped Silhouette.

Shirt body is proportionately tapered for comfort.

Cuff links are placed lower on cuff than is usual on standard models. Jewelry is small and inconspicuous.

All shirts have French cuffs.

Trouser legs are slightly tapered.

All hose for suits to be worn over the calf, with or without garters.

A variety of leathers and colors is available. The Demi-boot, strapped or plain, is most important.

Trousers are cuffless. Bottoms are cut on an angle to show maximum amount of footwear.

Shirt collar is higher in back and front for a bold, aggressive look...in tab and semi-spread styles.

Tie is slightly wider from throat to tip, with the widest part measuring $3^{1}/_{8}$" at bottom. Proportioned to tie handsomely into all shirt collar styles.

Handkerchiefs are of imported silk. Are designed to complement "THE TOTAL LOOK" in color and pattern, not to match tie or shirt.

Coat vents on single-breasted styles have a great deal of fabric overlap. Double-breasted models have scissored side vents.

Length of shirt reduced for maximum comfort and a minimum of fabric.

Suit trouser pocket is a full, quarter-top pocket; sport slack has a full top pocket.

Suit jacket slightly longer in length.

Trouser rise, for both suits and slacks, is slightly lower than standard. However, this must in no way associate the "Hardy Amies Look" with the very low rise "Mod" or "Hipster" styles of past seasons.

All trousers are belt-looped. Belts, therefore, are very important to "THE TOTAL LOOK" concept. Suit belts are of plain black or dark brown leather. Sport slacks have solid-color fabric belts only. All belts feature a gold-colored buckle.

Footwear features a pitched heel and broad toe to emphasize the forward "TOTAL LOOK."

WHAT IS THE HARDY AMIES U.S.A. TOTAL LOOK?

From head to toe.

STORE NAME

WHAT IS THE HARDY AMIES U.S.A. TOTAL LOOK?

STORE NAME

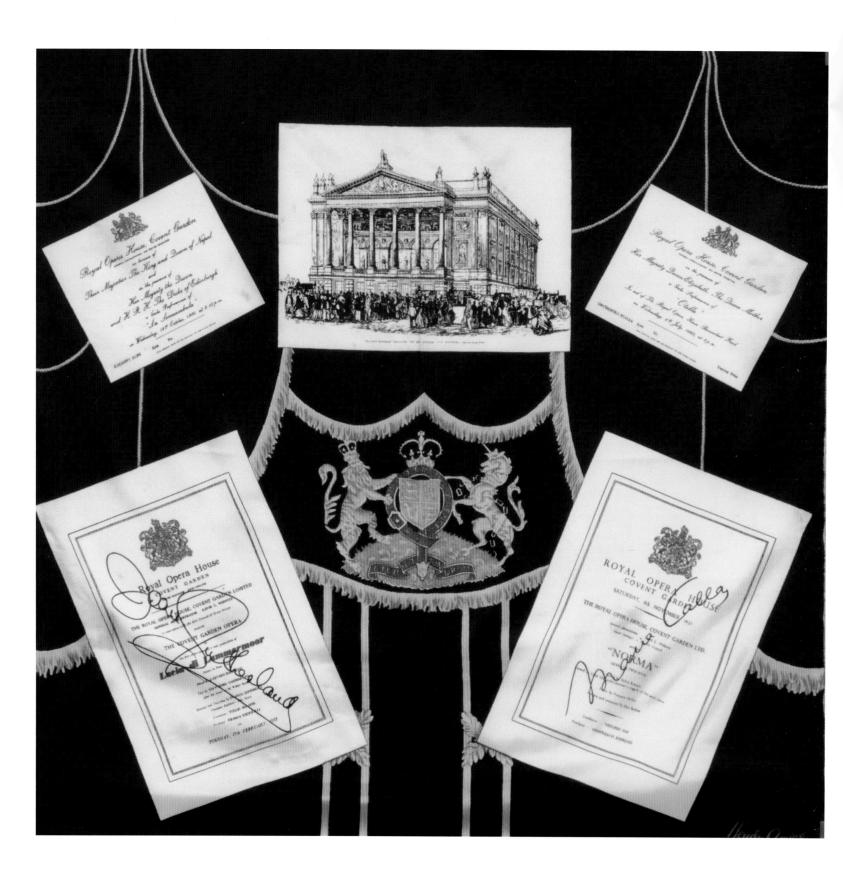

Opposite page: 'Opera', a design particularly associated with Amies and his Warrant as Dressmaker to HM The Queen, and which combined his love of eighteenth-century engravings and the Royal Opera House, where he formed friendships with the director David Webster and Joan Sutherland, amongst others. Winter 1959.

Right: In April 1959 the Hardy Amies Boutique began to sell scarves. 'The scarf is the perennial among feminine fashion accessories. It has grace, with a casualness which is correct with modern fashions. It is one of the best ways in which to add a colour note to a plain ensemble.' Amies said, when Kenneth Alexander Partridge arranged a display of them at the Alpine Gallery, London. (Umtali Post 15 May 1959)

Top: 'English Rose' designed by Graham Sutherland (1903-80) the artist particularly famous at the time for his tapestry in the new Coventry Cathedral. Amies bought several works by Sutherland, including a painting which formed the centre-piece of his Eldon Road drawing room.

Below left: A Hardy Amies scarf with a geometric design retailed in Japan and made there under licence of locally woven superfine wool as a fashionable winter accessory, circa 1978.

Below right: 'Firebird' designed in 1959 by Graham Sutherland, who also designed for Sekers.

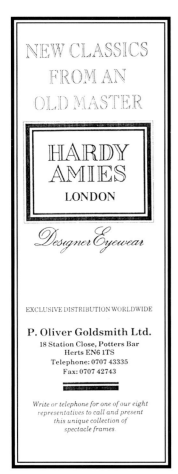

The design team in 15 Savile Row worked with manufacturers to produce lucrative accessories, such as spectacles and watches in the 1970s.

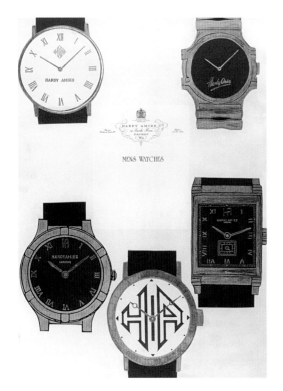

Amies was soon well ahead with his own plans for expansion through diversification, and was rewarded by the growing sales of his ready-to-wear label.

In 1959, he began discussions with Hepworths, a leading ready-to-wear men's retail tailoring manufacturer with branches in most British towns and cities, and shortly afterwards he signed a contract to design menswear. This was a complete departure in design for a famous couture figure, just pre-empted by Pierre Cardin in Paris in 1958. Other merchandising ventures soon followed. In 1960, he stated, 'I may not be as good a designer as many others, but I am more clear-headed and vocal.' (*Cape Argus*,

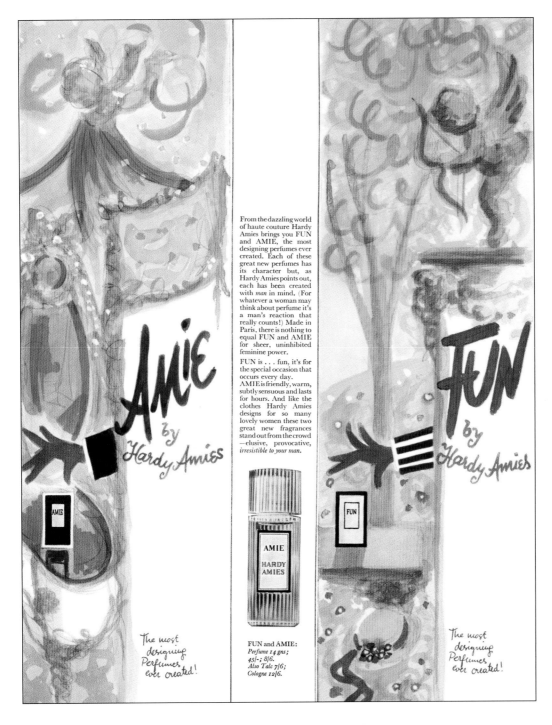

From the dazzling world of haute couture Hardy Amies brings you FUN and AMIE, the most designing perfumes ever created. Each of these great new perfumes has its character but, as Hardy Amies points out, each has been created with *man* in mind. (For whatever a woman may think about perfume it's a man's reaction that really counts!) Made in Paris, there is nothing to equal FUN and AMIE for sheer, uninhibited feminine power.

FUN is . . . fun, it's for the special occasion that occurs every day. AMIE is friendly, warm, subtly sensuous and lasts for hours. And like the clothes Hardy Amies designs for so many lovely women these two great new fragrances stand out from the crowd —elusive, provocative, *irresistible to your man.*

FUN and AMIE:
*Perfume 14 gns;
45/-; 8/6.
Also Talc 7/6;
Cologne 12/6.*

28 September 1960) 'Madame [sic] Chanel is an extraordinary woman and a great designer, but even she doesn't have the objective view. Chanel designs clothes for Chanel.' (*Minneapolis Star*, 4 October 1960) In October 1960 the first of the major restructures of the business took place as Brenner Industries manufacturing company Hardy Amies–Grosvenor Street was sold to Hardy Amies Ltd, and Hardy Amies Ready-to-Wear Ltd. In 1961 Amies sold the ready-to-wear business to the huge Selincourt textiles group, retaining artistic control, 'My couture house is the heart of the whole thing. And from it, and my thinking there, all other things spring naturally. They are just an extension of my work and it is the only way a couture house can survive to-day.' (*Sunday Times*, 16 July 1961).

Hardy Amies noted that even scents bearing the name of defunct couturiers continued to sell worldwide. In 1958 he registered and marketed 'Amie', 'Fun' and 'Hardy Amies for Men'.

Hardy Amies the Merchant

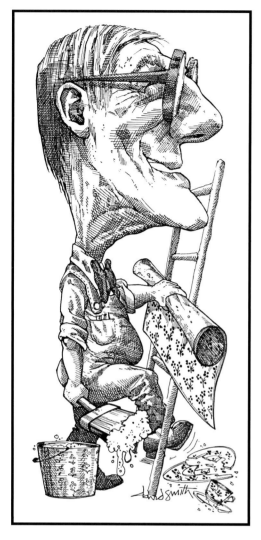

In 1973 Hardy Amies became part of the Debenhams group and the design studio at 15 Savile Row was financed to develop designs for household products, such as sheets, curtains and other textiles, bathroom accessories, somewhat rustic tablewares and wallpapers manufactured by Crown, satirised here (top left). *All tastes were catered for with varying success* (bottom left and top right).

In 1964 another British company, Battersby Hats, formed a design association with Hardy Amies to boost the declining popularity of men's hats, as a younger consumer market was altering the whole ethic of clothes design. Amies took a pithy view, 'Quant's 'Youth Look' is a great pace-setter – it's even influencing couture. I personally love the carefree philosophy of kooky designers. I wish they had more feeling for quality and fabric – but I suppose their clothes are supposed to look as if they're dropping to bits.' (*Flair* interview with Jean Rook, 1964) Perhaps coincidentally, Amies was awarded the Silver Medal of The Royal Society of Arts in 1964.

By 1965 Hardy Amies menswear was in Australian shops, 'You Australian men are such he-men you can get away with outrageous styles, without anyone clobbering you' (*Sydney Sun* 14 November 1965) The annual visits to Australia continued for decades. In August 1978 he told *Vogue* Australia, 'I don't know what Sydney thinks of me, but I'm really in love with him. Sydney is a chap. Sydney's most famous lady is Edna Everage. And he's a chap.'

Even tiles were designed and marketed under the Hardy Amies name. This 1970s pattern of tulips, one of his favourite flowers, was used by him at home in Langford, Oxfordshire.

In 1966 Amies signed another design agreement with Leicester-based Byford Knitwear, in order to re-vivify their staid designs which were failing to sell. In Canada, where a licence agreement with menswear manufacturers Copley, Noyes and & Randall was signed, it was noted that he looked '...an odd mixture of Alec Guinness and Noel Coward, and designs clothes for his kind of figure'. (*Montreal Star*, 3 November 1968) This observation came as a bemused comment after he had just signed a US$125,000 annual agreement with the important American GENESCO company to provide designs for men's clothing. He looked nothing like the average North American's idea of a businessman from the mainly Jewish clothing industry. The favourable UK press reports couldn't resist an occasional sting in the tail, '...if he swam the channel, he would step ashore immaculate ...[of INCSOC members] he is the most arrogant and mischievous.' (*Daily Mirror*, 1968) It was a frequent perception that he loved to trade on, and, once again, he had the last laugh: in 1985 GENESCO generated sales of over US$15,000,000 under the Amies label. (*SH* p.126)

The Amies look was also commissioned for a variety of uniforms including (top left) the British 1972 Olympics Team, (top right) the 1975 Oxford University Boat Club Team and (left) the 1975 uniforms for the London Stock Exchange Guides.

Hardy Amies commissions for the design of uniforms included those for staff working for liners, catering companies, the Hilton Hotel, London, the South African military, including the Army and Air Force and most famously, stewardesses of BEA 1967. Those for BA of 1974 were used until 1977 when Concorde came into service.

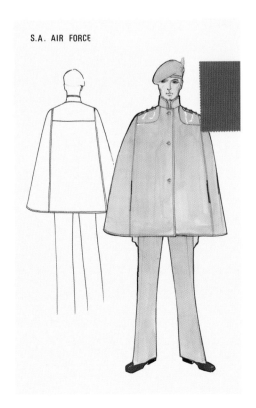

S.A. AIR FORCE

S.A. AIR FORCE
THEME 1. Airman

Hardy Amies the Merchant

In 1973, on the advice of Amies' advisor Eric Crabtree and chairman Sir Anthony Burney, Debenhams Ltd bought Hardy Amies Ltd intact for £525,000. In the process the backing from Hepworths was paid off, as were all the remaining shareholders of Hardy Amies Ltd. Amies retained one third of the business. (E. Crabtree obituary, *SH* pp.70-71) Debenhams' expanding empire of stores imposed an overall corporate-run structure and the necessary financial backing to each of its acquisitions, to the benefit of everyone within the company for as long as the relationship lasted. Amies stated that it was a wonderful relief to have this freedom from worrying about money and administration: 'Debenhams sent their own staff to Amies'. His loyal company secretary since 1946, Stanley Cox, was one of those now able to retire with a decent Debenhams pension.

In 1980 Debenhams relinquished many of its assets during a UK economic slump and Amies sold or borrowed what he could, in order to buy back his own business at a substantial discount, 'Ken Fleetwood says we are no longer Debenhams, we are Freebodies'. (*Observer* interview with Anne Boyd, 3 February 1980) At this time there were forty Hardy Amies Ltd licences in operation worldwide and the re-acquisition of the business was far more complicated than Amies had envisaged. The Amies designers and workforce were required to contribute much hard creative thought and work in the years to come – without the financial cushion of Debenhams. Never personally cash rich, Hardy Amies had finally benefitted from the ongoing changes to the company begun in 1973.

Some years later, he said of the re-acquisition, 'It was a much more difficult operation than I thought it was going to be, but now things are looking rosier, so I thought I had got something serious to leave... My only family is a sister, who is six years younger, who is of modest desires and throughout the years I have made her independent. There are private possessions which I have which she can have, so she's very happy with the concept.' (*Evening Standard*, 16 July 1984) He told another reporter 'I shall leave the company to my employees... Chanel dropped dead at 87 with a mouth full of pins. I never put pins in my mouth.' (*The News, Indianapolis* 20 July 1984) In the event, he survived until the age of 93, having witnessed the untimely deaths of first Ken Fleetwood and then Rosemary, before selling the company.

In 1964 Hardy Amies commemorated his links with Essex by designing the various robes worn by members of the University of Essex. Top: Lord Butler of Saffron Walden (1902-82), the first Chancellor of the University from 1966-82 with (below) the design for the chancellor's robes in Essex red, of Ottoman silk woven at Sudbury and the gold-plate lace woven on a Jacqmar loom to a traditional design; the mortar board in red silk with a gold bullion tassel. Britain's oldest robe makers, Ede & Ravenscroft, were consulted on various aspects of the cloth and design.

Hardy Amies was the recipient of a number of awards from the fashion industry including the Harper's Bazaar Trophy in 1962 (right), on a set (below) devised by Kenneth Alexander Partridge, designer of many INCSOC shows and interiors, including work for Norman Parkinson. Amies also received The Caswell-Massey International Award in 1962, 1964 and 1968; The Ambassador Magazine Award in 1964; the Sunday Times Special Award in 1965; The International Best-Dressed Hall of Fame 1974 List; 'Personnalite de l'Annee' (Haute Couture) Award 1986 and The British Fashion Council Hall of Fame Award 1989.

Chapter Ten

GLAMOROUS WEDDING DRESSES

Hardy Amies

Glamorous Wedding Dresses

Previous page: *The marriage of Lady Caroline Montagu-Douglas-Scott to future politician Ian Gilmour on 10 July 1951 provided Hardy Amies with his first great opportunity to display his skills as a designer in the ultimate religious setting of Westminster Abbey and in front of a large congregation, including several members of the Royal Family. The youngest daughter of the 8th Duke of Buccleuch was a niece of the then Duchess of Gloucester (2nd right from the bride). The Duke of Gloucester stands to the right of the bridegroom behind HRH Princess Elizabeth, now HM Queen Elizabeth II. Seated front left is her mother HM Queen Elizabeth, then Queen Consort of HM King George VI and (right seated) is HM Queen Mary, widow of HM King George V. Standing far right is the Earl of Dalkeith, later the 9th Duke of Buccleuch. They are assembled in one of the Robert Adam-designed rooms of Syon House, Isleworth, near London, belonging to the Duke of Northumberland, who had married the bride's elder sister Elizabeth in 1946. The day before this wedding, HRH Princess Elizabeth had visited Hardy Amies at 14 Savile Row for a private view of his current collection and would no doubt have taken a keen interest in the design and craftsmanship of this wedding dress. Later that year she ordered several designs from Amies, so beginning five decades of patronage.*

Left: *Lachasse was known for countrified clothes, primarily suits, when Hardy Amies joined in 1934. After a year or so, he began to introduce more day and evening dresses to the collections with beneficial results. His younger clientele were encouraged by his talent and the lower prices of Lachasse clothes. Some wedding dresses were commissioned from him, such as this example displaying the Amies pre-occupation with stripes and pleats to the rear of the skirt. The leg o'mutton sleeves indicate a heightened interest in the fashion of 1900. Circa 1937.*

Opposite page: *The marriage of Miss Ann Barlow to the Hon. William Bethell, son of 1st Baron Bethell, took place in the highly fashionable St Margaret's, Westminster. An interest in Regency styles for interiors and clothes was also fashionable in the late 1930s. This Lachasse-Amies dress of ivory peau d'ange silk had a smocked yoke to the bodice embroidered with glass crystal beads. The unadorned dress is in the Amies manner with a simple bias cut leading to the train. The bouquet was termed 'streamlined', like the dress.*

When Hardy Amies joined Lachasse in 1934, it was a business almost exclusively devoted to the design and making of elegant women's suits, still termed 'sports' clothes, because they were largely worn at sporting events. His predecessor there, Digby Morton, was amongst the first London designers to gain fame for creating such suits in a more urban style, yet the small Farm Street off-shoot behind the larger business 'Paulette' in Berkeley Square was so unknown outside sporting circles, that Amies had never heard of it. Before his interview, he travelled on the Sunday from his parents' Essex house to Mayfair and viewed the premises from outside. They were friendly in scale, rather than impressive, and he learned nothing about the business until his interview.

LAST WEEK'S LOVELIEST BRIDE — MISS ANN BARLOW.

MISS ANN BARLOW looked really delightful when she married the HON. WILLIAM G. BETHELL last week at St. Margaret's, Westminster. He is the younger son of Lord and Lady Bethell, of Bushey House, Bushey, Herts; and the bride is the only daughter of Major R. G. Barlow (late the Seaforth Highlanders), of The Holt, Ledbury, Herefordshire, and Mrs. Barlow, 33, Queen's Gate. Her gown was made of ivory peau d'ange, on Regency lines, and the smocked yoke was sewn with crystal. Her streamline bouquet was of Eucharist lilies and camellias. After the reception at Claridge's, Mr. and Mrs. Bethell left for a honeymoon in the U.S.A.

Above: *The Duchess of Buccleuch was an enthusiastic and considerate client, always popular at Hardy Amies. Winston Churchill once commented that when she entered a room, it lit up.*

Above right and opposite: *The marriage of Miss Jane McNeill to the Earl of Dalkeith, eldest son of the 8th Duke of Buccleuch took place in St Giles Cathedral, Edinburgh on 10 January 1953. As with the 1951 wedding, Amies designed a voluminous, full-skirted silver thread lace dress with an integral train to stand out against the space of the Cathedral and impress another notable congregation including the as-yet-uncrowned Queen Elizabeth II, who arrived in the Royal Train from Sandringham with her husband the Duke of Edinburgh and sister Princess Margaret.*

The Lachasse clientele was varied, as it turned out. Most clients would buy their day or evening clothes from one of a number of flourishing couture houses in and around Mayfair and often order their country clothes from the less expensive Lachasse, but that did not mean that the quality was reduced. Because of the lower cost and the increasingly fashionable wear of smart countrified suits in London, many Lachasse clients were also young. As soon as Amies was appointed Design Manager in 1935, he began to give his designs an individual stamp, not least in the construction and choice of materials. In discussions with the expanding clientele he had noted that Lachasse also had a potential market for day-dresses, blouses and evening clothes, which proved successful when introduced into the increasing number of models in each Lachasse collection.

Before 1939 fashionable Society weddings were usually held in London, attracting large crowds of onlookers to gaze at the equivalent of today's celebrities, known to them from the press or cinema newsreels. The fame and income of the larger couture houses was enhanced by London weddings, as the bride's dress and trousseaux were accompanied by

orders for not only the bridesmaids, but also family members or friends. A wedding was a way of securing ongoing custom and free publicity, so the elegant ingenuity of a wedding dress design was as crucial to the designer as it was to the bride. Until the outbreak of war in 1939 London hummed with social activity and every event demanded the correct dress. Mayfair, the area around Lachasse, was largely residential, as neighbouring Belgravia still remains. Both were particularly busy during 'The Season', a period of several months lasting roughly from the autumn opening of

Glamorous Wedding Dresses

Right: *A slim Amies wedding dress promoting the heavy Sekers-manufactured white double-duchesse satin of which it is made. In his collections of the period, Amies liked a slimline dress amongst the full-skirted designs of the period, knowing that they always sold well. This dress is worn by Susan Longfield, one of the in-house models, who later married cricketer Ted Dexter. Circa 1958.*

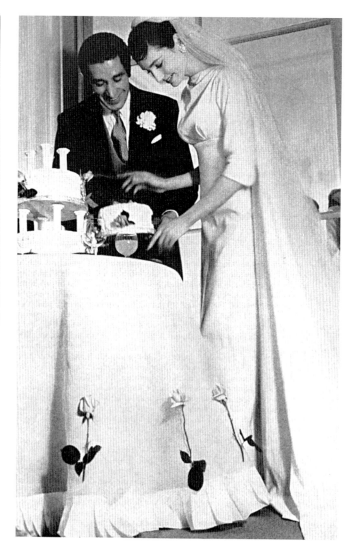

Right: *Hardy Amies always designed unique wedding dresses for clients, until the idea of ending a new collection show with a wedding dress became standard couture practice around 1960. The exception was advertising commissions, the first being for a rayon manufacturer in 1949. This example dates from 1950 and advertised table-ware.*

Below: *A sketch for the wedding dress of Lady Rosemary Spencer-Churchill, a daughter of the 10th Duke of Marlborough, who married Charles Muir on the 26 June 1953, twenty-four days after she was a maid of honour at the Coronation of Queen Elizabeth II on 2 June 1953. The Duchess of Marlborough was another influential and loyal client revered by Hardy Amies.*

Parliament until the end of June. This still followed a calendar established by the monarch and revolved around the activities at Court, including presentations of debutantes before the King and Queen at Buckingham Palace. Events during The Season were of particular commercial interest to designers and their suppliers, as well as ancillary trades and others involved, including photographers. As well as events at Court there was a continual round of parties and dances, mostly recorded in the 'Court & Social' columns of the broadsheets and many glossy magazines.

Amies was fully aware of all this, as he accompanied the young daughters of Mr and Mrs ffrench to various dances and parties. No doubt some of his fellow guests also became clients, and by 1939 Lachasse designs were noted in the press reports of Court Presentations. Each debutante had to conform to a prescribed code of dress, with long white gloves and the obligatory three feathers worn on the head, with a veil and a train behind. Amies was adept at finding novel twists to the fashionable lines of the dresses worn by both daughters and their mothers. A consequence of this was a number of orders for wedding dresses, and his identifiable designs of the period display the same preoccupation with the elimination of unnecessary detail found in his suits and dress designs.

Hardy Amies and Alexis ffrench's devoted member of household staff, Vincenzina, leaving the church after her marriage. The beautifully cut mid-1950s wedding dress was designed and made for her at Hardy Amies Ltd as part of her wedding present. The newly married Mr and Mrs Barrie Daniels looked after Amies for several years at 22 Eldon Road, London.

During the war, wedding dresses were still made in accordance with the restrictions of rationing, but no Hardy Amies designs are known from this period, when he carried on a skeletal business during his service with SOE. Nor do they appear to have formed much of his business in the post-war years, when he was establishing Hardy Amies Ltd, although he was commissioned by Marshall Field of Chicago to design one for the St Luke's hospital charity dress show in the autumn of 1947:

'It was very flattering that they should have chosen me from the whole of the Paris and London couture. I had some chalk-white satin specially woven by Warner's of Braintree, and as it was to be an autumn wedding I thought it would be chic and original to have the bridesmaids dressed in matt brown jersey as a background to the gleam of the satin. White flowers were to be used in bouquet and head-dresses to link the whole thing together. When I arrived in Chicago I found that the fashion show was to be staged in a huge arena as big as the Albert Hall... I was horrified to see my two bridesmaids coming solemnly on to the stage quite alone. I had completely forgotten that in America the bridesmaids arrive before the bride, so the whole effect was quite pointless. In the lighting, too, the dark brown looked black, and the head-dresses which I had imagined to be little coronets of white flowers, were made of white carnations, closely bunched together which resembled nothing so much as mortar boards worn rather awry. The wedding dress was not so hot, either; certainly not good enough to counteract this unfortunate entry. However, everybody was very polite, and the show was so huge and contained so many good things that my little effort was quickly forgotten.' (JSF pp.139-40)

Top left: Hardy Amies talking to Miss Shuttleworth, the daughter of the managing director of Hepworths, manufacturers and purveyors of men's ready-to-wear suits, with whom Amies had forged a highly successful business partnership in 1959. The full skirt of the Amies dress features a train and is balanced by the dramatic head-dress. Circa 1962.

Bottom left: The marriage of Miss Janet Bryce and the 3rd Marquess of Milford Haven on 17 November 1960. A first cousin of HRH the Duke of Edinburgh, he was the Best Man at the Duke's marriage to HRH Princess Elizabeth, now HM the Queen in 1947. The bride wanted an ultra-simple dress, and the Amies design reflects the unadorned bouffant outline that had superseded the full and more rigid crinoline design of such dresses in the 1950s.

Opposite page: A wedding dress for a special collection shown in the early 1960s, featuring a heavily ribbed material cut to form the spare shaped sleeveless fashion of the period as a wedding dress, apparently held together by shoulder bows, a favourite Ken Fleetwood device. The head-dress reflects the flowered helmet shapes of contemporary hats, and the elegant long gloves balance the sleeveless design. Circa 1963. The finale of the show including this dress is illustrated on p.259.

Glamorous Wedding Dresses

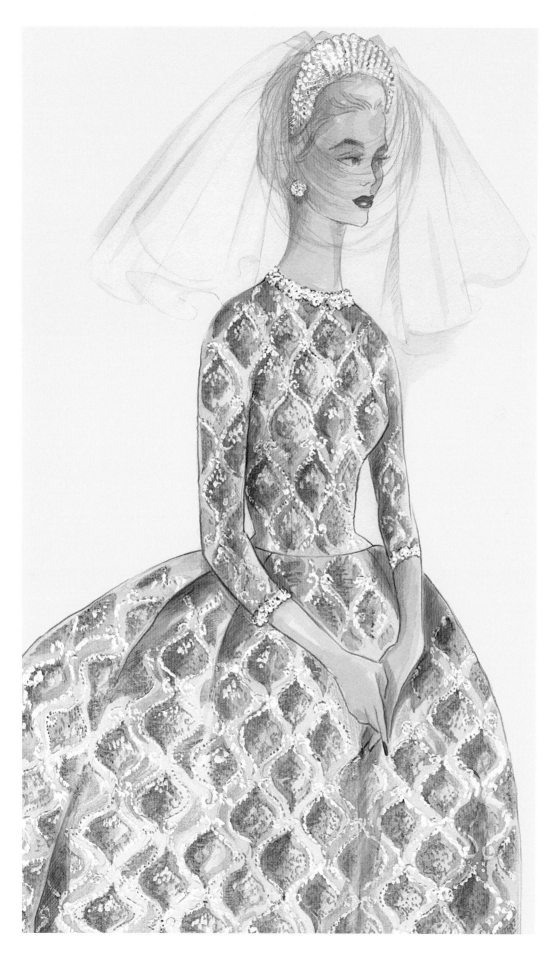

A Hardy Amies design of the early 1960s featuring a heavy brocade bouffant dress worn with a short veil attached to an impressive diamond tiara. The design epitomises the individual nature of giving a couture client something unique and memorable for a wedding dress. Circa 1962.

Opposite page:

Top left: The final touches during a fitting for a glamorous Amies wedding dress worn with a short veil in the early 1960s. The expertise of the workroom is evident in the finished dress.

Top right: Miss Zia Foxwell on the day of her marriage to Mr David Kruger, on 1 October 1968. The Amies design featured a slim dress overlaid by embroidered lace used for the long sleeves and falling in folds to form a train at the back and worn with a veil.

Bottom right: The parents of the bride, Major Ivan and Lady Edith Foxwell, for whom Hardy Amies designed a fashionably short gold brocade mink-trimmed dress. Blending the dress of the family with those of the bride was and is a usual practice for a couture house.

Ending a collection with a wedding dress was a later couture innovation that developed into a tradition, and although his desk diaries record the appointment of major clients he wished to see, only two relate to wedding designs. The Amies press books of the period first include a wedding dress design in 1949, made as publicity for a rayon manufacturer. The faded newsprint shows a full-blown Edwardian revival dress incorporating a peplum and modified bustle, much in the style of some of his evening dresses. Unsurprisingly, there are no images of the St Luke's Show dress. Amies was undoubtedly lucky that his first experience of designing a wedding dress for a very large space took place outside Britain, which was to become the scene of his greatest wedding dress triumphs in a few years time. By 1951 matters had changed.

Reflecting in his second volume of autobiography *Still Here* in 1985, Amies wrote, 'I have been involved with the making of many wedding dresses over the past fifty years. Such orders were always treated with loving care, not always matched by the parent's willingness to spend money. "After all, it's only for one day", the landowners rich in acres but rather pressed for cash would say. There has now been a marked change in attitude.' Amies dearly loved a Duchess, for many reasons, and they responded to him. 'Two patronesses who were impeccable in their behaviour as regards money and totally inspiring in their enthusiasm for our designs were the Duchess of Marlborough... and the Duchess of Buccleuch, who brought all her daughters to us for wedding dresses including Lady Caroline, who married Ian Gilmour (in 1951). She also brought us her future daughter-in-law and the future Duchess, the very beautiful Miss Jane McNeill.' (*SH* pp.152-53)

Three Amies-Fleetwood designs for wedding dresses of the mid- to late 1970s, sketched by in-house artist Jackie Marks. The designs epitomise the pared-down lines of the time, but have a romantic appeal in the full skirts of one and the demure simplicity seen overall.

Miss McNeill typified a short-lived post-war trend for a well-bred daughter to take a job as a house model in a couture business. She became well-known for her work, mainly with Norman Hartnell, and married the heir to the Duke of Buccleuch, the Earl of Dalkeith in January 1953. 'We made a dress in silver lace, very plain as to detail, very bold in outline' Amies wrote. 'Skirts of crinoline proportions were very fashionable. We gave one to the bride and allied it with a very simple bodice and long tight sleeves. The lace was so stitched and appliquéd that there was no break in the line anywhere. It was magnificently simple and simply magnificent – helped, of course, by the bride's beauty and elegance of figure. She was crowned, literally, by one of the Buccleuch tiaras. There were several to choose from.' (*JSF* p.153) After the wedding the dress was later altered into an evening dress and lost the integral train.

Right: *The marriage of Miss Elizabeth Servaes to the artist Timothy Fargher on 15 July 1978 at St Bartholomew's Church, Orford, Suffolk. Photographed during their reception at The Old Rectory, Orford, the bride wears a full-skirted soft ivory coloured dress with an integral train and an equally full veil, designed by Kenneth Fleetwood with reference to Hardy Amies.*

Below: *Victoria Mathias married Anthony Jarvis of Doddington Hall, Lincolnshire on 25 July 1962. Her romantic dress was designed by Neil Roger, then an investor in Hardy Amies Ltd. He ran his business as 'The Sheridan Room', located in Amies' former office to the right of the main entrance on the ground floor. Roger's designs were executed by the Hardy Amies Ltd. workrooms.*

The Buccleuch connection also led in time to another order for a wedding dress, for the next generation of the family, when the son and heir of the marriage, in his turn the Earl of Dalkeith, married Lady Elizabeth Kerr, 'This time it was Ken Fleetwood's turn. His dress was as different as could be from mine for the previous Lady Dalkeith... It was based on a design of about 1880. The dress of white taffeta had a skirt draped back into a bustle, the draperies held by bunches of white roses.' During the wedding service Ken said to me, "We've got very grand seats; we are just behind the family and, I think, in front of the cousins." I replied, "It's a bit like *Upstairs, Downstairs*." "Can't think what we are," said Ken. "We're not upstairs and we're not downstairs; I think we're *entresol*." ' Typically, Amies later qualified his praise with the wry comment, 'When the bride appeared I felt considerable pride that a pupil of mine had made such a beautiful wedding dress', as though Fleetwood had not been doing so for over quarter of a century.

Apart from an oblique request made to Hardy Amies and then described to Jon Moore, for designs for a 'wedding dress for a country wedding', which later turned out to have been for the wedding of Lady Diana Spencer to The Prince of Wales, the only royal wedding dress order was for HRH Princess Michael of Kent. A simple cream silk suit was made '...in a great hurry. She wore it for the civil wedding ceremony in Vienna in 1978 and again at the validation service in London in 1983... Princess

Flocked organza and embroidered
wedding dress with satin bows.
Tiered skirt with tight, fitted
bodice and sleeves worn with
short veil scattered with tiny
bows.

HARDYAMIES

Above, left and right: *A discreet enquiry for wedding dress designs for a 1980 wedding was given to Jon Moore. The only instruction he was given was that, 'it is for a country bride from a good family'. Only much later to his annoyance did he discover that the discretion had masked the identity of Lady Diana Spencer and that no such country wedding was intended – far from it.*

Left: *Jon Moore with Miss Sulaimanian wearing his Hardy Amies romantic full-skirted design with a sweetheart neckline, puffed sleeves and a full veil. Circa 1982.*

Above and left: *The front and rear of a full-skirted Kenneth Fleetwood design, with an embroidered bodice and back, specially made for a licensee, featuring a full veil. Circa 1986*

Below: *The marriage of Lady Elizabeth Kerr to the Earl of Dalkeith, later 10th Duke of Buccleuch, on 31 October 1981, the bride followed the Buccleuch tradition by ordering her wedding dress from Hardy Amies, designed by Kenneth Fleetwood.*

Michael is a customer who had done us many kindnesses and leads the applause at our dress shows at Savile Row. The Princess has a professional eye for clothes which she chooses with great care. Not for the first time am I glad that our clothes last. They have to be of great use to the very busy Princess Michael who is exceptionally photogenic.' (*SH* pp.152-53)

When Hardy Amies and Ken Fleetwood went through the design archive at 14 Savile Row around 1990, they destroyed most of the designs not connected with work for the Queen, so little survives of the many individual wedding dresses made over the preceding decades. In any case, full designs in the traditional manner were not usually made after the 1970s. Jon Moore followed Ken Fleetwood's lead in sitting with a client and sketching ideas in front of her, until a mutually satisfactory design was achieved. Sadly, almost none of these survive and the photographic archive is also thin. Many images remain anonymous.

Above left: *The marriage of Miss Cressida Hogg to the Hon. Henry Legge, a son of the 9th Earl of Dartmouth and Raine, Countess Spencer, on 21 December 1995. The bridegroom's mother had been a faithful Hardy Amies client for decades. The wedding dress with a low scooped neckline and skirt with soft gathers was designed with the muff by Jon Moore, who also designed the dress of her mother Lady Hogg.*

Above right: *The marriage of Lady Charlotte-Anne Monatgu-Douglas-Scott to Comte Bernard de Castellane on 14 September 1991. The daughter of the 9th Duke of Buccleuch, the bride wore an Amies dress with a gently scrolled neckline and a softly gathered skirt.*

Hardy Amies was always fascinated by the effect of his designs from every angle and paid close attention to the back of a dress. This design by Kenneth Fleetwood for a full-layered dress, overlaid by a swathe of material extending into a train beneath a dramatic veil, is firmly in the Amies tradition. Unfortunately, as with so many images in the archive, the identity of the bride is now unknown. Circa 1992.

Amies summed up his own attitude to the design of wedding dresses in his amusing *ABC of Men's Fashion* of 1964 (reissued in 2007), 'As a couturier I have dressed many brides; and through the courtesy of their mothers, have attended many weddings. I am also old enough to have seen many of my friends and their daughters married. It is always a day of tension. Parents display exactly their social position: for relations are on view. Bride and groom wonder what their future is going to be. Dressmakers, florists and caterers pray that they have done their part well; it is a day on which even they do not feel blasé.

The least one can do is to see that the clothes are as helpful as possible. It requires first of all a little clear thinking. It should be remembered that all are guests of the bride's parents. Furthermore, it is the bride's day. It is, therefore, for her to decode what sort of wedding she wants. No-one will accuse her of extravagance if she wants a long white dress.' He also deals in detail with what the bridegroom should wear and under 'Honeymoon' he warns 'See *Holidays* and be doubly careful.' (*ABC of Men's Fashion*, p.122)

By the mid-1960s the display of a wedding dress had become the traditional stunning finale to the showing of a couture collection. This show took place at the Hilton Hotel, Park Lane, London, for which Amies designed new uniforms for all the staff in 1963 in collaboration with the manufacturers of Terylene, and Amies himself stands on the steps at the far left. The wedding dress is illustrated on page 251.

Chapter Eleven

ODYSSEY FROM STAGE TO 2001

Hardy Amies

Above left: *In August 1948 ballerina Margot Fonteyn was one of the Sadlers Wells Ballet Company, including Pamela May and Beryl Grey, who set off for the USA with a complete wardrobe furnished by members of INCSOC. The press was enthusiastic, and wholly perceptive of the dollar-earning capacities of such a scheme. Margot Fonteyn is modelling the Amies grey suit and a swing-back black fur-lined jacket called 'Snuggle' made of Irish tweed.*

Above right: *Hardy Amies basking in his admiration for the musical glory of Maria Callas and Benjamin Britten in the mid-1950s. The diva was not known as an Amies client, nor is there any record of this promising event.*

Previous page: *The mid-1950s was undoubtedly the high-point of British couture, promoted abroad by the glamour of the young Queen Elizabeth and a remarkable number of photogenic members of the British royal family. The twelve main INCSOC members were further patronised by elegant women from around the world, also home-grown and international stars, who would visit the daily in-house showings of the latest collections and often encounter friends and colleagues, as here in November 1955. Hardy Amies expounds a detail in his showroom to British stars (left to right) Mary Hayley Bell (Mrs John Mills), Vivien Leigh (Lady Olivier) and Phyllis Calvert.*

It would have been natural if Hardy Amies had become famous for costume designs, as he had early on shown great aptitude as an actor in his Brentwood school productions. As all couture designers of his generation were adept at staging their in-house showings of their own collections, which almost amounted to mime, very many were called on to dress stage or film productions and some, such as Dior with Marlene Dietrich or Givenchy with Audrey Hepburn, became associated with the glamour of these stars. In London, Hartnell and Stiebel were associated with the most glamorous of the British stars and stage or film productions and delighted in their company.

Hardy Amies also had a good number of actresses amongst his clientele, especially after his connection with Princess Elizabeth became even more famous after she succeeded to the throne in 1953. His American film-star clientele grew enormously from the days of the late 1930s, when the then Lady Jersey first ordered her clothes from Lachasse. She was Virginia Cherrill, famous for her Hollywood role as the blind flower seller in Charlie Chaplin's 1931 film *City Lights*. She made few films, apparently saying that she was not a good actress, and became Mrs Cary Grant in 1934, divorcing him in 1935 and marrying the 3rd Earl of Jersey in 1937. A staunch supporter of Amies and one of his first backers in 1946, Cherrill unfortunately divorced Lord Jersey the same year. When she re-married shortly afterwards, she and her new husband went to live in America. It was through her that other Hollywood actresses, such as Mildred Shay 'The Pocket Venus', became clients. Vivien Leigh, one of the greatest stars of the period became a regular client and Amies often escorted her to first nights and parties.

Vivien Leigh was one of the world's superstars, when she was first dressed at Hardy Amies in the 1940s, with Gone With The Wind still a potent symbol of her beauty and talent. Although he often accompanied her to first nights and dinner parties, and was frequently photographed in her company, Amies omitted her name from both of his autobiographies. In a 1996 interview with Angela Lambert he said, 'Vivien Leigh was a great beauty with tremendous taste. I remember one collection we showed a very simple dress in navy blue and Vivien said: "I want it in black." I said:"Oh, no, please don't. It'll look dowdy in black." But she said: "No, I'll have it." When it was made up, Odette, her personal fitter, said "Voila, Madame," and she said "I think I'll give it to my mother." She was an arch-bitch!' She is seen here in the Amies showroom appraising a sleek evening dress in Coronation year, 1953.

Although it may seem curious that Amies never considered a career as an actor after his school successes, part of his character clearly rebelled against what many film actors have found aggravating in the repetitive nature of the stage work. Ian Garlant, a former Amies in-house designer maintains that Hardy was always acting and that he was an egocentric, surely not bad attributes for the stage, yet the quest for fame and fortune stretched his talents in other directions through design and business. When he discussed his work within 14 Savile Row, he compared his role to that of a conductor, not a stage director.

In his book, *ABC of Men's Fashion* he writes under 'Theatre', '[that it] is, of course, much less important than opera. The same rules apply [for dress] but need to be enforced less stringently; except for plays by Shakespeare, Congreve, Sheridan, Wilde, Shaw, Wesker and Pinter.' (*ABC of Men's Fashion* p.113) It should be noted that he had acted in works by the first three playwrights at school, and perhaps thought that he had seen enough. However, this flippant nonsense is expanded upon by a statement made years later, 'Apart from dressing a few famous actresses such as Edith Evans when she was given a role of a lady who, in character, dressed as one who would patronise a *couture* house such as ours, and the delicious job given us by Glyndebourne to dress Kerstin Meyer in an opera, in which she played the richest woman in the world, we have never done much work in the theatre.'(*JSF* p.142) This lack of theatre work is even more curious, when one considers that Ken Fleetwood was passionate about theatre design early on.

Having stated his opinion on the superiority of opera over theatre in his *ABC of Men's Fashion*, Amies only ever designed for one opera, the 1974 Glyndebourne production of, 'Der Besuch der alten Dame', (The Visit of The Old Lady) in three acts by Gottfried von Einem, to the libretto based on the play by Friedrich Durrenmatt. The Swedish mezzo-soprano Kerstin Meyer created the role of the old lady, Claire Zachanassian, in the British premiere at Glyndebourne in 1974.

'The Old Lady' was an ideal Amies character, as she is intended to represent the richest woman in the world, but is more than unconventional with her retinue which includes her husband, a butler, two servants, and two blind eunuchs, as well as a coffin, a caged black panther, and a large amount of luggage. The Amies designs do full justice to the familiar Rhineland surroundings of a small town in the opera and a person not too unlike some of his clients in terms of purchasing power. Although

Dame Edith Evans, a faithful client on and off stage for almost forty years, here wearing an Amies dress, possibly in Bernard Shaw's, Aerial Football or The Black Girl in Search of God (also by Shaw) at the Mermaid Theatre in 1968. Although they clearly had a rapport, Amies was happier discussing opera with client and friend Joan Sutherland or music with her husband the conductor Richard Bonynge. The few surviving notes in the Amies archive mainly relate to questions of Dame Joan's dress and her account with the instruction not to let her husband know how much she had spent with him.

Kerstin Meyer, Swedish mezzo-soprano, in the first British performance of Der Besuch der alten Dame by Gottfried von Einem at Glyndebourne in 1974. The role of the multi-millionairess Claire Zachanassian called for an extravagant wardrobe and it was ordered from Hardy Amies, who was not only familiar with the surroundings of a small German town, but also the type of Parisian clothes favoured by the German rich. An annual visitor to Glyndebourne and a patron for a time, he was also a star guest at a legendary Foyles Literary Luncheon for the launch of a celebratory book on the opera house in May 1984.

superficially a comedy, it is a forceful opera about the corrupting power of money. Amies also drew on his knowledge of the type of clothes worn by the fashionable in Germany. He probably also thought of his Kenya-based client Lady Delamere, who was always particularly welcome at Savile Row; very often she ordered more clothes in a season than the Queen.

On the subject of opera and clothing, Amies wrote in *ABC of Men's Fashion*, 'It is too banal to say that you went to opera before the War to be seen rather than to hear the music. But it is certain that you dressed up for it. Today [1964] I notice a band of faithful who look perfectly correctly dressed. Their enthusiasm for opera is balanced by their sobriety of dress. True, there are usually two gentlemen in opera cloaks and tailcoats of rather bizarre cut, and, I suppose, toupées. But they have at least made an effort. It must be recorded, however, that the rest look pretty crummy. I think it all goes back to the days of austerity, when Covent Garden first opened. We now have an opera house of international reputation. Our standards of music are international. We could not do better than to copy international standards of dress. On first nights you wear a dinner jacket; on other nights a dark suit. Nothing else will do… A different standard applies to Glyndebourne. The journey is a pilgrimage, your attendance a ceremony.'

Hardy Amies went to Glyndebourne every year for at least two or three performances from the late 1940s onwards, always taking a companion, very often Nina Leclercq during the 1950s. Hardy Amies Ltd was a patron for a short time, as were other friends of his such as Miki Sekers of Sekers Fabrics. Another friend, Martin Battersby designed productions and Amies became friends with many musicians, performers and conductors, especially George Solti. He genuinely loved opera for the intensity of human expression he found in the vocal, instrumental, and design elements of a production.

The plays for which Amies designed are thinly sprinkled across his post-war career. The designs and any images of the costumes have largely vanished. In 1948 for Sacha Guitry's farce *Don't Listen Ladies* at the Theatre Royal, Brighton, Amies designed for the blonde beauty Moira Lister who performed as the wife of a Parisian antique dealer who had suspicions about her behaviour. Curiously enough, years later Lister married a Frenchman and became the Vicomtesse D'Orthez.

In 1949 at the Winter Garden Theatre, Anne Hayes wore Amies designs in the play *Top Secret* as did Joyce Redmond in the 1951 production of *Count Your Blessings* at Wyndhams. Also in 1951, Edith Evans was dressed by Amies in *Waters of The Moon* at the Theatre Royal, Haymarket. 'Apparently, Dame Edith Evans rescued N.C. Hunter's 1951 wintry drama from Binkie Beaumont's slush pile, and it ran for two successful years in the West End' was *The Guardian* critic's patronising comment on the 2004 Salisbury revival. (*The Guardian*, 26 January 2004)

Part of the honour of having Dame Edith Evans as a private and professional stage client brought about the same problem encountered by Norman Hartnell with Queen Elizabeth, The Queen Mother. Both had a glorious style of their own, but no one else could or would emulate them. The honour was enormous, but the resulting business negligible.

2001: A Space Odyssey, directed by Stanley Kubrick and released in 1968 has become a cult classic. Much of the atmosphere of the space flight interiors depends upon the clothing worn by the actors. Kubrick commissioned the designs from Hardy Amies in 1965.

Top left: Dr Floyd is set for his on-board meeting wearing a Hardy Amies jacket.

Above: A design for a 'man in the crowd', one of the famously deleted scenes from Kubrick's masterpiece. The colouring, texture and type of materials are not too dissimilar from those used in the Hardy Amies menswear designs of the period, especially the flap to the top pocket and the small collar to the high-buttoned front.

Left, centre: Near the beginning of the epic flight Dr Heywood R. Floyd (left) played by William Sylvester, goes through a voice identification process to gain clearance and access to the space craft. His clothes were not unusual then, nor are they now, proving Amies' theory that predicting future fashion as a radical change of style can be nonsense.

Left: A design for the tunic jacket of 'Captain Bishop', presumably the Aries-IB Lunar Shuttle Captain played by Edward Bishop with various changes indicated to the detail and colours, usually made after meetings between Kubrick, Ken Fleetwood and Michael Bentley, head of menswear for Hardy Amies Ltd.

Inventive designs for mothers and scientists. The colours and shapes again similar to contemporary ones, with some novel shoes included. Shoes were to be made by the leading London shoemakers and retailers, Rayne of Bond Street, who were consulted by the Amies designers. The dress above right is an abstract op-art Bridget Riley- influenced pattern for a dress worn by a young mother in a deleted scene.

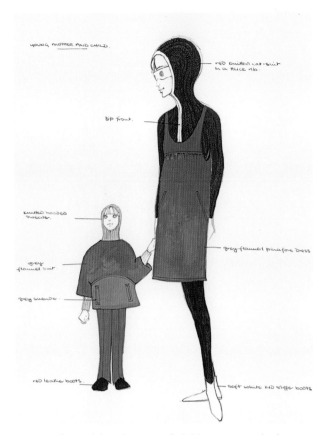

Designs for a deleted scene of children in a park, the designs and colours reflecting those for teenagers and young women of the mid-1960s.

Like Hartnell, Amies was a proven master of dressing people with style in settings akin to theatre, whether in cathedrals for weddings or on varied State occasions. In this context the next play Amies dressed is appropriately named. The 1951 production of *Affairs of State* by Louis Verneuil at the Cambridge Theatre, starred Joyce Redmond again dressed by Amies in yet another French farce; he was becoming typecast for such design. There was a break of ten years (according to the Amies press books) until Amies dressed Vanessa Lee for a 1961 British production of Norman Krasna's sophisticated Broadway hit comedy, *Kind Sir*, already the subject of the 1958 film *Indiscreet* starring Ingrid Bergman and Cary Grant, with whom Amies later became friendly in Hollywood.

Dame Edith Evans also wore Amies' designs in Robert Bolt's unsuccessful 1963 comedy, *Gentle Jack*, co-starring Kenneth Williams, who later reminisced that Dame Edith complained to him about Binkie Beaumont instructing her that as Hardy Amies had made her very regal clothes, she should wear them accordingly. She was not amused. For her almost her last appearances during 1973 and 1974 in *Edith Evans and Friends*, she was again attired in a glorious Amies dress of brocade.

Hardy Amies participated in very few film projects, although he often went to the cinema with friends, just as he did the theatre. Instead, he designed

Odyssey from Stage to 2001

Above: *One of the early scenes on board the space transport of Stanley Kubrick's cult classic film of 1968, 2001: A Space Odyssey, depicts the stewardesses attending to the few passengers on board. Fururistic touches include an apparently microwaved tray of food being served, whilst the wide-screen television shows one of the many BBC channels beamed from earth. The uniforms are by Hardy Amies and the helmets made by Frederick Fox. This is the last recorded film on which Hardy Amies worked.*

Below: *The stewardess exits the kitchenette with a tray of food, heated in the oven. Curiously, almost everything depicted in the film has dated and closely resembles designs of the period in which the film was made, proving Amies' point that predicting future design is a risky business.*

for stars' personal wardrobes, beginning with his days at Lachasse where clients in 1939 included the British film star June Duprez, then famous for her role in *The Four Feathers* and later *The Thief of Bagdhad*. Post-war clients included Constance Cummings, then famous for her role in the David Lean film of Noel Coward's *Blithe Spirit*. Other American stars such as Marlene Dietrich, Linda Christian, Pola Negri, Hedy Lamarr, Paulette Goddard, Ava Gardner and Ginger Rogers all came to see collections, and many bought from them. In the 1970s Amies designed for Ginger Rogers' London stage performance in *Auntie Mame*. British stars Phyllis Calvert and Margaret Lockwood were clients, as were Margaret Leighton and Evelyn Laye, but his work was rarely commissioned for films. However, In 1955 the celebrated British film costume designer did use the Hardy Amies Ltd workrooms for the clothes she designed for Margaret Lockwood to wear in the film *Cast A Dark Shadow* co-starring Dirk Bogarde. Amies allowed her to bring in her own designs and Miss Lockwood was in any case a private client of his firm. This practice of utilising couture workroom expertise was formerly widespread for British films, *and was a useful means of extra work for the fashion house,* but was a form of business which never seems to have been utilised at Hardy Amies Ltd, mainly because the workrooms were always operating at full capacity until the mid-1970s.

His first film credit came in 1949 with the lavish Herbert Wilcox vehicle for his wife Anna Neagle, *Maytime In Mayfair*. The thin musical storyline is woven around a Mayfair couture house and the showing of a small London collection includes the Amies coat featured on the *Vogue* cover of March 1949, when worn by Norman Parkinson's wife Wenda Rogerson. Apart from Amies, clothes by Charles Creed, Norman Hartnell, Mattli, Molyneux, Digby Morton, Bianca Mosca, Peter Russell and Victor Stiebel are the fellow INCSOC members featured, so it was hardly an Amies triumph.

Until 1960 Amies was involved with few films, but in that year he dressed Deborah Kerr in *The Grass Is Greener*, again co-starring Cary Grant involved in a romantic triangle and directed by Stanley Donen who became a friend of Amies. The next commission came in 1962 with designs for Joan

Greenwood in the film of the play, *The Amorous Prawn*, another gentle British comedy, followed in 1965 by the far tougher plot of Agatha Christie's, *The Alphabet Murders*. In this film Tony Randall, as Hercule Poirot, was dressed by Hardy Amies, a reflection of the new status enjoyed by Amies as a distinctive name in menswear design, a success repeated with designs for Albert Finney in the 1967 film, *Two For The Road*. Directed again by Stanley Donen, the film starred Audrey Hepburn, dressed by Mary Quant, Paco Rabanne, Michele Rosier and Ken Scott. Neither her favourite designer Givenchy, nor Amies, were chosen for what was a romantic film about a young couple trying to rekindle a marriage.

In 1965 some Hardy Amies designs are credited as worn by Patrick Macnee to wear as John Steed in the cult television series, *The Avengers*. The collaboration did not last: Steed later wore suits by Pierre Cardin, amongst many other designers used.

The next Hardy Amies film design commission came in 1965 from Stanley Kubrick, known for his wit and intelligence in treating complex and emotive themes on the screen. *2001: A Space Odyssey* is now regarded as a significant milestone in film history, and has an immense cult following, together with an extensive literature surrounding it. Kubrick was fully aware of the Hardy Amies name not just as a designer for the Queen, but also of menswear. He had settled in Oxfordshire with his family and was planning *2001*. In his second autobiography Amies wrote about this time:

'I must record, however, the wonderful time that Ken Fleetwood and I had working with Mr Stanley Kubrick on his famous film *2001*. Our role on that film was to design clothes for a period in the future. The film, released in 1968, meant that we were dealing with a period thirty-five years ahead in time. To try to get a perspective on this I looked back over the previous thirty-three years to see what had happened in the world of fashion. I realised to my surprise that there had been less change than one had imagined. I didn't foresee, therefore that clothing in the year 2001 would be dramatically futuristic.'

Quite how Amies came to this conclusion is difficult to understand, as the clothes of the 1940s had nothing in common with those of the mid-1960s, although those of around 1930 did bear some resemblance in the simplicity of line. Amies went on, 'Mr Kubrick accepted this. There came a moment, however, when we had to discuss the clothing of the Russians. These he wished to appear as dowdy and old-fashioned, "Right", we said, "we'll put them in the clothes of today." This, of course he couldn't accept. Nor could he accept our suggestion that the astronauts should wear disposable underclothes. "Oh, no," he said, "I shall have every housewife in the audience wondering if she has made a mistake in ordering a new washing machine." (JSF p. 142) Viewers of the film might wonder just where the underclothes would have been shown, unless Amies meant the scene in which the astronaut David Bowman (played by Keir Dullea) is seen exercising in white boxer shorts. In retrospect, the dresses of the visiting Russian scientists, and the costume of the lead scientist, played by Leonard Rossiter, seem the least dated.

The receptionists' uniforms are particularly interesting, as Hardy Amies had previously been commissioned to design several uniforms for women as diverse in nature as factory workers at Walls ice-cream factories, Lyons restaurant waitresses and air hostesses. There are resemblances in these 2001 uniforms to those of the BA stewardesses designed around this time.

HA S
o.k'd by S. Kubrick.

DR. BOLAND

A1
STAR OW
22476

Above: Three inventive designs for the film with examples of unusual hats and a sleeveless draped shift over blue slightly-flared trousers, possibly meant to have been worn with a draped skirt. Below: Three examples of innovative shoes to be worn by women in a scene either never shot or cut.

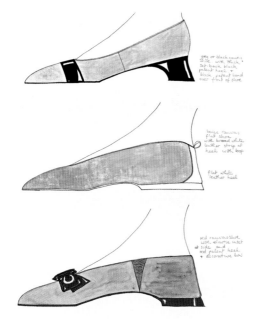

Strangely, there are no entries in Hardy Amies' visitors' book, desk or pocket diaries relating specifically to appointments with Kubrick. The 1965 desk diary has the entries 'October 4 : 2.30 MGM' and on Friday 8 '2.00 MGM here – models' (amusingly followed by 'Gotterdammerung' Amies' evening at the opera). Next, on Monday 18 after lunch at the French Embassy is the note 'Film Studios', and on Saturday 23 Amies left the UK for the Far east returning in time for Christmas on 12 December. There are just two margin entries in pencil from the 23 and 30 March 1966, 'Ken to Banbury Oxford', which reveal that Fleetwood was dealing with the film design, presumably involving Amies in discussions after the first meetings.

In October 1965 Amies gave an interview to the American journalist Eugenia Sheppard, 'The fashions aren't going to look too different in 2001... It's re-assessing... I'm doing about twenty designs for men and women in the film. The men are scientists and the women are doctors, space hostesses and secretaries. They aren't kids, in fact, most of them are around fifty... that means that the principals are today's fifteen-year-olds... most people's fashion patterns are set by the time they are fifteen. I am not gifted with any ESP... I know my fashion history. The formal end of fashion keeps disappearing. It's consistently being replaced by the category below. Ever since Edward VII started wearing tweeds for town... I've already picked some next century fabrics from DuPont, mostly, thick, but textured... I want fabrics that will give me a nice clean shape for photography. Nothing gauzy because of the no-gravity situation. I'll plan to do a one-colour look. By then we should have even more marvellous shades, I see clothes, shoes and stockings all the same.' The only part of the look he worried about was the then fashionable long hair, which would blow around, so he thought short hair would be worn – as it was. 'It's only thirty-five years away, and even if things change twice as fast, they can't change too much.' (*New York HT*, 31 October, 1965)

Twenty years later he wrote, 'I admire Stanley Kubrick enormously, and I think his film is still one of the most exciting ever made. He was, however, very bad at explaining what he wanted. I don't think he was always sure of this himself. He certainly made it plain to us when we presented anything to him which he didn't want. I cannot resist telling, rather mischievously, a final story. There are in the film several airlines travelling to the moon, to Mars and to other planets. When I suggested that each airline should have its staff in different uniforms, Mr Kubrick said, 'Oh no, in the year 2011 all airlines will be owned by PanAm!' (*JSF* p.142)

Amies spent much of 1966 abroad, and Fleetwood was in regular communication. On Monday 8 November 1966 he wrote in his usual erratic style, '...the film people have been giving a little trouble, at the same time we move along but it is hard and slow progress and he will keep changing the designs alas not for the better I fear... (Ken flew back from Paris)... just to fit the film people and found one girl had been thrown out of the film whilst the other girl hadn't bothered to keep her appointment... I am now on to mothers and children and... still cannot quite see how the action will unfold heaven alone knows what we will be in for.' On 19 November 1966 he wrote again, 'The film has been hard work but I think they are really pleased with them although they have had too many sketches for what they really need. I think that now Kubrick has real confidence in us and the tensions are less. Mike [Bentley, in charge of Amies menswear] and I went out the other afternoon and got a great deal settled I found just the right boots for them and now I am working with Rayne on the other girls shoes. Mike was a great help, an early acting career certainly helps even if he did look and act like Archie Rice of the Mens Clothing Industry.' (letter to HA) Ken apologises to Hardy Amies for his hasty typing and urges him not to forget that Hardy is still a womenswear designer, whilst soaking up international praise for the menswear ranges.

From this, it is clear that Ken Fleetwood and the in-house designers share the artistic laurels for everything done for *2001* together with Frederick Fox, who was responsible for the hats. Fox remembers (in conversation with the author 2012) one typical filmset occasion concerning one of the immaculate white suede hats worn by the stewardesses. The actress had been reading a newspaper, but when called back to the set, jumped up and put on her hat, leaving two beautiful black ink hand prints on it. 'Cut'.

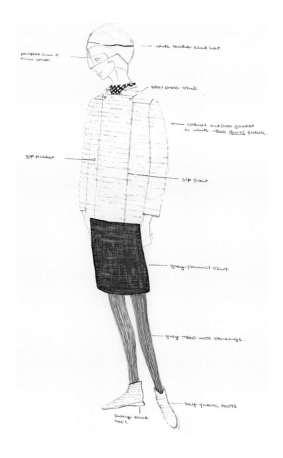

Right: The fruition of the Kubrick collaboration with Hardy Amies was ultimately not as rewarding as the designs indicate, because many of the scenes in which most of the finished clothes were to be seen, never appeared on screen and would clearly have had quite an impact.

Chapter Twelve

HARDY AMIES
FOR MEN

Hardy Amies

Hardy Amies for Men

Previous page: *A dynamic view of Hardy Amies-Hepworths suits, featuring the type of evening wear seen on page 279, with swirling capes, and topped with Battersby hats. Circa 1966.*

Right: *In the USA, Hardy Amies capitalised on his business and social contacts to spread his menswear ventures. Hollywood royalty, the film star Edward G. Robinson was universally well known for his tough characterisations of both good and bad guys. He was also a serious art and antique collector, delighting in entertaining interesting people, not just the Hollywood movie crowd.*

Below: *Elegant friends Hardy Amies and Jonny Witte stroll through a park in the typically sporty style of German menswear around 1930. In the 1970s Amies re-introduced the blazer to his collections.*

Opposite page: *Leaping in the park, thirty-five years after his German stroll, the 1966 Hardy Amies-Hepworths menswear style was photographed in Savoy Gardens on the Embankment, London, outside the Savoy Hotel, where the fashion shows took place. Following the June 1961 press conference, the first show of twenty-five garments was held in September 1961, Amies receiving the Harper's Bazaar Award for outstanding achievement in creative design.*

For a time in the mid-1960s Hepworths Hardy Amies ready-to-wear suits were the most fashionable for aspiring young British dressers, ironically in a way that none of his womenswear suits ever were. In 1966 the English Football Team won the World Cup and their smart off-field suits were designed by Amies. There could hardly have been better publicity at a date when British men of all classes regarded a suit as the smart thing to wear for anything more than a very casual event.

By 1950 Amies had already sensed that income from couture was not capable of sustaining a company of the size of Hardy Amies Ltd and this prompted his astute move into ready-to-wear clothes, both for export and for sale in the new in-house Boutique. In 1953 he added men's ties to the Boutique collection, much as he knew Dior had done, considering that Amies' clients would be able to give the men in their family an item bearing the Amies name, although they failed to sell in quantity. He ordered ties made by the 'four-in-hands' method from a folded silk square from Michelsons, famous for their ties, and in 1961 set up a formal association with Hans Wallach of Michelsons to

Above: *Hardy Amies practising what he preached on menswear to the world. A commanding and dapper figure encased in a fashionable loud checked suit of the period standing outside 14 Savile Row. Circa 1968.*

Right: *A rare surviving approved menswear design for a Hepworths suit of the 1960s in the Hardy Amies Archive, bearing the comments and instructions of Amies to his designers. Circa 1966.*

produce Amies ties and sell them world-wide, and in June 1961 he became linked to the design of a range of Hepworths men's retail ready-to-wear suits. (*SH* p.65, *The Tie* p.7)

Hardy Amies had always been interested in men's clothing. He badgered his mother for a dinner jacket when a teenager and photographs of his days in Germany are marked by his chic clothes. In 1990 he clearly remembered being nine years old (1918) and precociously reading E.F. Benson's, *Mammon & Co*, so strong a memory that seventy-two years later he sought out the book in The London Library and quoted, 'Kit had given him a charming turquoise of the *vieille roche*, a piece of noonday sky, and incapable of turning green. It would be suitable to wear that when he met her, but unfortunately it did not go at all well with his clothes. However, sentimental consideration prevailed, and he put the ruby back, pinned the turquoise into his tie, and looked at himself again. "It is rather an experiment" he said half aloud.' (*The Tie* p.6)

In his conversations with an old friend, the 'Queen of Bohemia' Viva King, he must have noted her own reminiscences of of her father, 'His Savile Row clothes became old, but they never looked it and were worn with the unconscious ease of an English gentleman.' (*The Weeping and the Laughter* p.37) From 1934 when he started with Lachasse, Amies himself had his suits made by Wyser & Bryant a traditional British tailors. (*SH* p.68) He addressed the similarities between men's and women's suits in 1954, 'A man's suit is psychologically a glorious comfortable thing. Even if you are a dandy and spend a great deal of time choosing your cloth and supervising its cut, once you have given attention to your dressing and toilet in the morning you need think nothing more of your dress – except to "adjust it before leaving" from time to time – until you take it off. I am sure that women have the same feeling with their suits… The most careful critic of such suits is the customer's own husband: "My dear, you can't wear that thing at Newmarket", he will say.' (*JSF* pp.172-73) The same came to be applied in reverse with Amies' designs for men's Hepworths suits and led to his dictum, 'A man should look as if he had bought his clothes with intelligence, put them on with care and then forgotten all about them.' Amies was always keen to experiment and his chance with menswear came with a telephone call from Prince Yuri Galitzine in 1959, as Amies wrote, although nothing much happened until 1960, according to his diaries. (*Still Here* pp.67-68)

The 1960s Hardy Amies menswear image: youth, speed, style. The pullover made by Byford and tie by Michelsons all carrying the Amies label. Circa 1965.

Hardy Amies for Men

Above: *The look of the late 1960s Hepworths ready-to-wear suits with Regency collars, as designed by Hardy Amies. The style has evolved from the design seen on p.276, especially the length of the men's hair, worn by twins John and Dennis Myers, whose fame at the time led to their appearance together as the von Meck twins in Ken Russell's 1970 film, The Music Lovers.*

Opposite page: *Playing to the same bemused street audience as above, the tight-trousered and satin-edged dinner jacket with an evening cape are redolent of the suave James Bond film character then capturing many imaginations, when dressing for the evening was an aspirational event for most young men. 1967*

Prince Yuri (Yurka) was a man calculated to arouse Amies' interest and confidence, not because of his ancient lineage and family connections, but more as a former Intelligence Officer in the Second World War. He had a distinguished war record. A former member of the reactionary group 'The Right Society', he witnessed French reprisals against young French collaborators and, disgusted by what he saw, was further horrified when he took part in the liberation of the Natzweiler death camp, one of the first camps to be entered by the Allies. He renounced 'The Right Society'. A survivor, the pre-war *Vogue* sketch-artist Brian Stonehouse, had sketched several of the murdered SOE women agents seen briefly in the camp. Galitzine swore to track down the murderers and was successful in keeping the SAS tracking unit going after it was officially closed in 1945. (*The Secret Hunters*, Anthony Kemp, p. 81) The resonance would have been felt by Amies and his friend, Nina Leclercq, manageress of the Amies Boutique, as her kinsman Michel de Brunhoff the head of French *Vogue*, had lost his own son to similar murderous elements of the German Occupation in Paris. In 1955 Galitzine set up his own successful public relations company, gaining clients such as P&O, and around 1960 he put Amies and Hepworths together – Amies liked to claim the date as early as 1959, but his diaries reveal 1960. There was some rivalry between the date of Cardin's own first catwalk show of male ready-to-wear and Amies'. Cardin was first.

Hardy Amies for Men

Master of showmanship and re-invention of his business, Hardy Amies stands on the catwalk with the latest men's and women's ready-to-wear designs in 1968. After a successful visit to his licencees in Australia, Amies continued his sales campaign in New Zealand, where the Cambridge Clothing Company of Auckland belonging to the Macky family sold Hardy Amies suits nationwide. It was claimed that Amies dressed over half the male population of New Zealand at this time. Whilst there, he was re-united with Howard Hayden, his retired English master, who had inspired him at Brentwood School in the 1920s.

Founded in Leeds in the nineteenth century, Hepworths had become a retail giant headed by Norman Shuttleworth, the managing director of three hundred UK retail outlets, who had grown up within the 'Fifty Shilling Tailors' business of Sir Henry Price, where Shuttleworth's father was managing director. It is difficult today to comprehend the scale of such businesses, but they and another Leeds competitor Monatgue Burton, known as 'the thirty shilling tailor,' each sold around eight million suits a year in the 1930s. The shop assistant would measure the customer, who chose the cloth from swatches, the suit came back for fitting and was then returned for finishing.

By 1960 men's clothes were changing rapidly under the twin influences of Italian fashion and Pierre Cardin's menswear interests, first seen in his 'Adam' boutique in the 1950s. Cardin's biographer dates the first catwalk show of his couture menswear as 26 February 1960, at the Hotel Carillon, with an audience of international press and

recruited Sorbonne students. The ready-to-wear men's designs made under a worldwide licence by S.A.M. Bril et cie were given a catwalk show on 7 July 1961. He quotes Cardin, 'The professional male model didn't exist then, we hired university students.' Like Amies, Cardin was famous for his women's couture, leaving Dior to set up his own House in 1950. The professional furore over his new menswear led to him being temporarily excluded from the Chambre Syndicale; of which INCSOC was a pale imitation. Amies mentions Cardin's menswear launch and claimed to have been first ever with a men's ready-to-wear catwalk show, but this applied to Cardin. He must have known; Galitzine, Shuttleworth and Eric Crabtree certainly did. (*Pierre Cardin*, pp.93-94 et seq.; *JSF* pp.67-69)

Eric Crabtree was, to quote a mutual friend of Amies, Derek Granger, a man with a '...mercurial personality and mesmeric gift for seizing attention, was a determined and successful businessman who possessed

Walking in Savoy Gardens, the models parade the latest Hardy Amies-Hepworths styles for casual wear. The suit on the far right is notable for Amies' own predilection for the late Victorian evolution of the high-buttoned suit jacket, here with an exaggerated wide collar derived from a version of the ghillie collar. Circa 1968.

Right: *Hardy Amies explains the new menswear designs to bemused members of the Hepworths board during the 1962 show at the Savoy Hotel.*

Below: *The 1966 Savoy Hotel catwalk show. The lightweight suits suitable for hot climates have ultra-slim revers, even to the double-breasted version, all emphasised by the dark glasses and fez accessories.*

that rare quality: enthusiasm. He personified the businessman who revels in his work and he flaunted his belief that commercial work should, above all, be fun. His attitude was a positive denial of weighted down boardroom glumness and confining strictures of corporate identity.' (*Daily Telegraph* obituary 19 September 1995). He also had a distinguished war record in the Royal Army Service Corps, founding the Royal Military College of Science. He much later went on to found a medical research facility with Dr Jean Shanks, Galitzine's second wife.

Amies had met Crabtree towards the end of the war and his diaries record regular meetings with him from then on. In some ways, he was an *eminence grise* to the Amies business, going with him to Yorkshire (where he was born) for the meetings with Hepworths and doubling the Amies fee in the resulting contract. Crabtree became a member of the boards of both companies and later became deputy chairman of Debenhams and brought Hardy Amies Ltd under their corporate umbrella. He was mistrusted by Ken Fleetwood, who found the cosy life at Amies being rocked. 'Eric is on the phone to nag because business is down, doesn't help, how can a man with a voice like that get on so well.' (*KF letter to HA* 8 November 1966)

Writing to Amies again in the USA in 1966, Fleetwood complained about Amies' letter to Crabtree, 'Despite the fact that you may think we all have nothing else to our day than drink coffee with Bunny (Roger), an idea I don't think you should have put into Crabtree's head, there are quite a few outlandish ideas there now without you adding to them. Had he started life in the men's trade I feel he might have picked up a little more about the working of this trade. I say this after having had one of the most pointless discussions with him in this office that I

Hardy Amies-Hepworths suits acquired even greater fame and cachet when in 1966 Hardy Amies designed the suits worn by the World Cup winning English football team. Pictured here are team captain Bobby Moore (centre), with Martin Peters (left) and Geoff Hurst (right).

have ever had. I sometimes fear his dreams are other people's nightmares. If he could remember from time to time that we all here at Savile Row still think of you as a womans [sic] designer too it wouldn't be a bad thing. As best they can the sales ladies fight on... We are all thrilled by your success (in New York with menswear business).' (*KF op cit* 19 November 1966)

Crabtree had other detractors. He had gained control of the flourishing Cresta silk shops in 1950, which had grown out of the heritage of Wells Coates, a Modern Movement-inspired architecture and design company. Patrick Heron, the son of the 1929 founder Tom Heron wrote, '...what did Eric Crabtree do? He ordered the burning of all Cresta blocks and screens and dismantled every surviving Wells Coates shop, installing in their place pastiche Regency pediments, columns and pilasters. Thus shops which had heralded the Modern Movement in architecture in Britain now looked like tenth rate eighteenth-century stage sets.' (*The Independent* 24 September 2004) Crabtree can be seen as an asset stripper, especially with the Debenhams drive to

Above left: *A co-ordinated and optimistic country outfit with a short coat worn over a three-piece checked tweed suit. Circa 1966.*

Above right: *The surviving caption reads, 'A three piece suit in mixed brown check stretch tweed. Single-breasted, three buttoned and buttoned flap Van Dyke pockets. Made-to-measure at £17.15.0d.' This was not inexpensive: todays' equivalent is £503, based on average earning power.*

purchase as many local UK department stores as possible throughout the late 1960s and early 1970s. When in-house, he also agitated Amies' devoted Company Secretary Stanley Cox, as witnessed by at least one former Amies employee. (*Geoffrey Angold interview* 2012)

After Amies had signed his contract in June 1961 with Hepworths, he consulted Mr Wyser, his own tailor, for critical design input. In order to overcome the board resistance to a male catwalk show of the new designs, a display was put on in Galitzine's house, 'By gum, we could sell these!' was one remark, and indeed they soon sold nationwide. (*SH* op cit) No doubt in honour of this, Amies took Galitzine and his wife to Glyndebourne on 18 June appropriately, in all circumstances, to a performance of 'Fidelio'.

The subsequent first public Amies-Hepworths show on 11 September 1961 at the Savoy Hotel has become part of UK fashion history and resulted in the additional benefit of Hepworths money being invested in

Hardy Amies Ltd, with a Hepworths director on the board, again organised by Eric Crabtree. (*SH* pp.67-69) The press coverage was enormous in the UK and abroad, especially in the Commonwealth, Amies making annual trips to Australia and New Zealand, and later Japan for the next three decades.

With the Hepworths label, now being put in clothing as 'Designed by Hardy Amies Hand Cut By Hepworths', Hardy Amies added to his fame in the early 1960s. He wrote a column for the mass-circulation American men's lifestyle glossy magazine *Esquire*, one amongst British literary giants such as Evelyn Waugh. His articles appeared amidst reports including the latest male fashions, cars, holidays and early 1960s aspirational information, all suitable for the recent television cast of *Mad Men*. This column grew into his 1964 pocket-sized style guide, *ABC of Men's Fashion*, an often delightfully quirky personal view of his subject, intermingled with useful advice or definitions of material names. For as many rules as he laid down, so he would subsequently break them. But the journalism and the book certainly gave him added kudos and fame. He also exchanged ideas with a new friend, the London tailor Tommy Nutter, who stayed with him in New York and was introduced to useful contacts. He and Mr (Michael) Fish were two of the new menswear successes of Swinging London, a changing fashion scene noted and adapted to the Amies style.

A subsequent 1966 Hepworths show included in the audience a director of the enormous USA clothing conglomerate GENESCO, formerly the Nashville shoemakers, General Shoe Corporation. This had been enlarged by Frank Jarman, son of the founder, into a mighty business empire, which ultimately foundered, as the Amies-Debenhams relationship did. Jarman later invited Amies to America for talks on founding the subsequent contractual relationship. Not everyone liked the new Hepworths designs. Amies himself struggled to convince the board to accept a purple suit, and further down the social scale, by 1974 a *Daily Mirror* journalist set up a review of Amies' new 'banana yellow *Great Gatsby* bags', inspired by the film starring Robert Redford. Shown to a group of northern miners coming off their shift, the results were not unexpected, 'Ah thowt thee were a bloody puff or summat', was one reaction and another from a man who wore the suit, 'I looked like a big band trombonist or chip salesman'. Another said, 'Is he daft this Amies feller? You wouldn't catch me in that', and another was equally forthright, 'Nay lad. Not for me. Maybe some of them Londoners – but they don't mind looking like puffs.' (*Daily Mirror*, 12 November 1974)

In any case, an Amies observation that fashion ultimately always ascended rather than descended the social scale was proved by the jeans revolution. It had arrived by the 1950s and was included in his

The classic look of a Hardy Amies country suit, high buttoned with slant flap pockets. Photographed outside 14 Savile Row. Circa 1966.

The smashing
sport coat,
designed by
Hardy Amies
of London

Known 'round the world
for his design and tailoring
talents, Hardy Amies'
sport coat features today's
new bold British
silhouette that fits and
flatters American men.
Sleekly cut with flapped
pockets and deep side
vents, we have it now
in a handsome collection
of town and country
fabrics. $000

STORE
NAME

*The fall/winter 1976 GENESCO advertising
campaign was as extensive as it was expensive.
This is a typical mock-up of an advertisement
promoting the British Hardy Amies style, the
tweed jacket with the fashionably large revers
and cap probably aimed at the Ivy League
market. Advertising was placed in* Esquire, The
New York Times Magazine *and* Playboy.

*The more conventional styles of a Hardy Amies
for Hepworths suit and shortie overcoat worn in
St James's Park by Rudi Patterson circa 1967.*

1964, *ABC of Men's Fashion*, where he noted that the cloth was supposed to have originally come from Genoa, hence the name, 'No single garment has ever had such an influence on the costume in general. We note, too, that it is originally a garment destined for working in, that has graduated into something for playing in, and then has influenced that shape of formal clothes. Jeans are more attractive when well worn, being of a cloth of a colour and texture which is improved by frequent rough washing, as are most peasant clothes: a sturdy symbol of democracy.' (*ABC of Men's Fashion* p.73) Unfortunately he did not spot the niche for designer jeans. Writing in 1972 he stated, 'Jeans give you a sense of freedom. You can wear them all week or all weekend. You can do anything in them. Just throw them into a bag and keep them clean. Young men look very athletic in them. Older men, if they don't look athletic in them, think they do.' He wore them himself: '...a t-shirt is the most appropriate thing to wear with jeans. These are body garments, they have influenced the whole of dress, they are making men extremely body conscious. Men's clothes are doing what women's have always done, making the body look younger, nicer and more athletic.' He then qualified his remarks by adding, 'This does not mean that a suit need be dull – and it is my job to see that it isn't.' (*The National Times* 30 February 1972)

At the end of the 1960s Amies and Jarman wanted a total 'Amies Look' at GENESCO, combining the many existing Amies contractual agreements with various companies, including hats, gloves, scarves, ties, shirts, socks, shoes, knitwear, pyjamas and suits, marketed in America. GENESCO mounted an extensive and expensive publicity campaign in the late 1960s for Hardy Amies Ltd in general, and in-store concessions in particular to promote the idea. David Harvey, Amies' in-house public relations manager from 1966-68 remembered the presentation to the men from GENESCO: 'Flanked by his directors and acolytes such as Bentley and myself he took over a banqueting room at Claridge's and regaled his American visitors with his philosophy and recipe for success – dramatically winding up with a glance at his watch and saying: "Now the soufflé is served." '

When Amies had first gone to meet GENESCO in the mid-1960s, his fame was already widespread in North America, fostered since his first post-war visits, and subsequently built on during regular trips and his international fame as a royal dressmaker. His competition in North America came first from Paris and a few American designers. Over the decades new American designers gathered strength, as did Italian; GENESCO had contracts with many of the leading names by 1970, but Amies remained in a higher category due to his royal warrant and his popularity in American society. His diaries show that he had first met the ultimate 'walker' Jerome 'Jerry' Zipkin on his first visit to New York in 1946 and Zipkin's name appears at intervals over the following decades. Doors were opened for Amies all over America. So much so,

Above left: A 1967 Hardy Amies for Hepworths 'Mid-weight Blazer Jacket in red and brown check solid worsted with plain brown slacks. Single-breasted, three brass buttons, patch pockets. Ready-to-wear jacket at £11.19.6d, trousers £6.12.6d.' Based on average earnings this is equivalent to £340 today.

Above: From 1967 'A shortie raincoat in white Terylene/cotton with red wool lining. Single-breasted, three buttons, ghillie collar, cuff buckles. Ready-to-wear at 9gns (£9.9s.0d)' Based on average earnings approximately £267 today.

Left: A 1967 'casual jacket in blue Terylene/cotton, with check tweed lining and matching tweed slacks. Zip front ghillie collar. Slacks have flap front pockets. Jacket ready-to-wear at £8.19.6d. Based on average earnings approximately £255 today.

that in 1968 Amies acquired his New York apartment at 68 East 68th Street and retained it until he died, spending large amounts of time there doing business, entertaining and being entertained.

Did he design all the menswear ranges himself ? No more than he designed all the women's clothes from around 1960 onwards. As with most great couture designers, he had assistants with whom he conferred, detailing his ideas and the type of fabrics required. The studios (then in 15 Savile Row) employed assistants and there were sketch artists. Ken Fleetwood was in charge of the womenswear from at least 1960, although not officially until 1982, and menswear was headed by Michael Bentley, a former actor and model. Amies was always involved with the creation of the collections in some way, examining and changing details or more, right up to the final conclusion of the making-up process. With menswear he evinced an obsession with the type and placing of buttons, perhaps even more than he did with women's designs. (*Harvey op cit*)

David Harvey experienced the uphill struggles with both Hepworths and GENESCO. 'The 'total Amies look' of the latter fizzled out, ironically to be taken up by a Hepworths renamed Next, offering packaged looks for men but dumping Amies on the way.' (*Harvey op cit*) In 1982 Terence Conran had become Chairman of Hepworths and George Davies became chief executive of the new Next company. 'Amies also experienced some hair-raising business accidents. Launched into the American market in 1969 with unprecedented ballyhoo by the former GENESCO conglomerate, he was obliged to watch as the US stock market shenanigans reduced the corporate giant to almost nothing, saw his label discounted, and play a cat-and-mouse game to try to resume his contract. By the time he recaptured his label America had grown its own squad of men's designers and the world wanted to dress American anyway.' (*Harvey op cit*) However, GENESCO survived and was still selling and promoting Hardy Amies in the mid-1970s.

Opposite page:

Above left: *A 1960 design for 'Hardy Amies Men's Wear by Radiac: "The Young English Look". A range of men's wear – shirts, collars, underclothes, pyjamas and dressing gowns – manufactured by Radiac. This dress shirt is in striped cotton voile, it has three pleats each side of the centre pleat. Note the rounded collar and cuffs. Retail price 75/-. The black satin evening tie is designed by Hardy Amies and made by Michelsons.' Based on average earnings approximately £211 today.*

Above centre and right: *Two 1960 designs for Hardy Amies Radiac shirts and Michelson ties aimed at young professional businessmen.*

Bottom: *Hardy Amies often travelled to West Germany during the 1960s, but never managed to break into the menswear market there with his British look. The West Germans had their own distinctive image of the period and sometimes the Amies designers hit it correctly, as with this maxi-coat of 1970, which seems to owe more to the bad old days than the land enjoying the fruits of the Wirtschaftswunder. In any case, the maxi look was a short-lived fashion for men and women.*

Right: *The sophisticated elegance Hardy Amies wished to project in all his menswear in the mid-1960s with the high buttoned dinner jacket and patent leather shoes giving the correct fashionable look.*

From the 1970s onwards, together with Roger Whiteman, the Amies label was re-merchandised and women's clothing was particularly successful worldwide. By 1995 there were some fifty licensing operations ranging from small leather goods to bags and various forms of womens and menswear. In his eighties, Amies continued to gain publicity.

In 1994, Amies published another book on a subject dear to his heart. *The Englishman's Suit* is a lively account of the origins of today's classic British suit and 'the ghillie collar' came to prove as enduring and obsessive a topic of conversation as 'The Winter Queen', moving Rosemary to comment on her ageing brother's posturing in one of the new Amies jackets, 'Just look at him, he looks perfectly ridiculous'. He may in her affectionate regard have momentarily seemed so, but she and everyone knew that to be far from the case. As he stated in 1973, 'In fashion today there are no old men – only the young and the dead.' (*Daily Mail* 25 October 1973)

Above: Colourful examples of the Hardy Amies knitwear designs for Byfords of Leicester tops, from the mid-1960s with the loose line of the blue-edged cardigan.

Right: In 1968 Hardy Amies had a lucrative contract with Bonsoir nightwear to produce a colourful range of varied garments, as seen here. This was another instance of Amies wishing he could have a completely co-ordinated Amies range produced by one company.

Bonsoir PYJAMAS

AMBASSADOR — Luxurious satin stripes. *Approx. retail price 84/-.*

REGENT — The two tone look designed by Hardy Amies. *Approx. retail price 63/-.*

RALEIGH — Look, no buttons! *Approx. retail price 49/6.*

TSAR — The Zhivago look designed by Hardy Amies. *Approx. retail price 63/-.*

The Hardy Amies **SLEEPCOAT** — The ultimate in sleepwear *Approx. retail price 49/6.*

cotton

Left: *Mid-1960s Hardy Amies designs for silk ties and scarves made by Michelsons in an amusing setting. The silk was no longer exclusively made in Britain and as the mills closed, so the firm turned after the mid-1960s increasingly to Como, Italy for their supplies.*

Below: *During the 1960s Hardy Amies had a contract with Clarks shoes to produce innovative men's footwear, including suede versions of the war-time Desert Boot and leather boots given a fashionable boost in the wake of the nostalgia for Old Russia created by the success of the film Dr Zhivago and the defection of Rudolph Nureyev to London. He favoured even higher boots. The design of the elastic-sided boots emulated their Edwardian predecessors, but Amies gave them a Cuban heel. As with the Byfords knitwear, Amies insisted on the best quality and regularly travelled to the Clarks factory.*

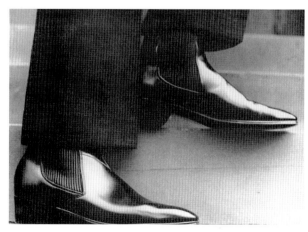

POSTSCRIPT

THE EVOLUTION
OF THE NAME

Hardy Amies

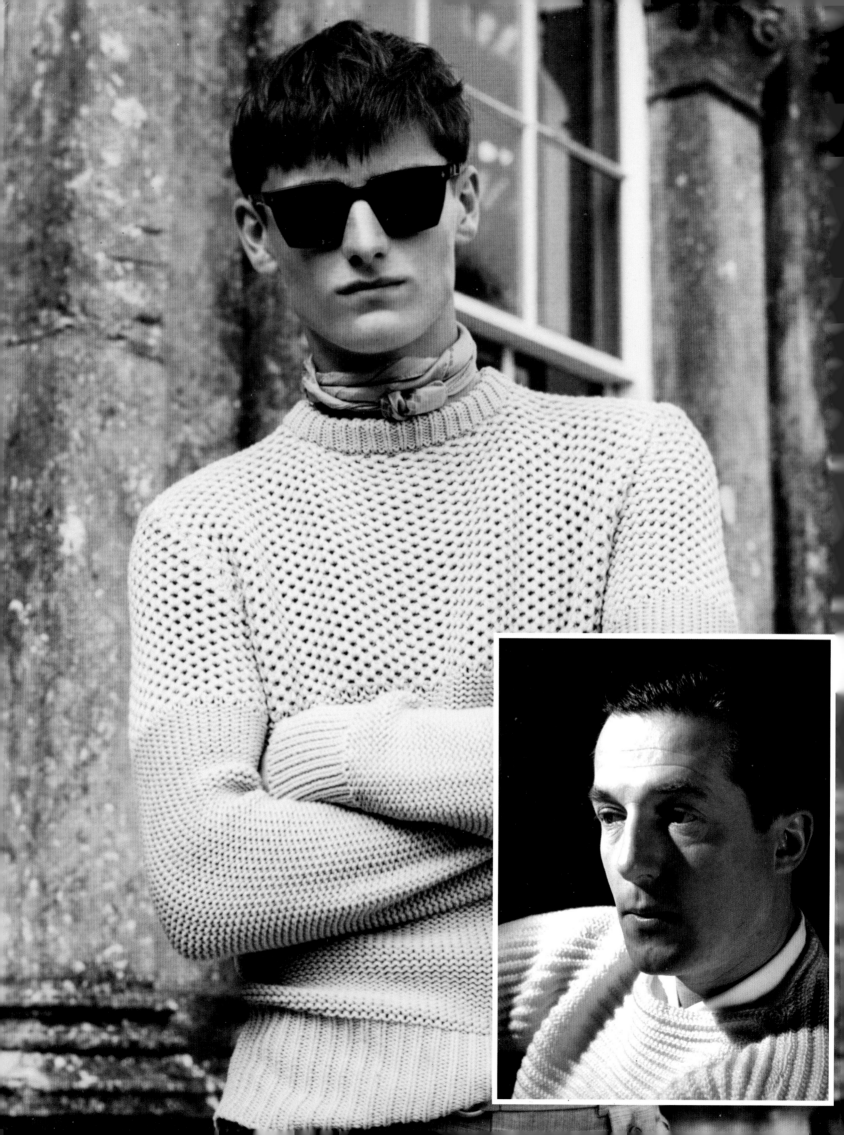

Great names in fashion often outlive their founders by means of a judicious mixture of inventive design in the hands of a new designer willing to re-assert the characteristics of an established look and with effective merchandising of the name.

Hardy Amies had hoped to be able to leave his business to his workforce as a going concern, but increasingly found himself in need of extra income after he had reached his ninetieth birthday in 1999. His younger sister Rosemary and his chief designer and colleague for over forty years Ken Fleetwood both predeceased him, and he had to plan for an uncertain future. The business was sold in May 2001 and Amies died in March 2003. After a period of valiant changes of ownership, which included the acquisition of the Norman Hartnell name, the company was acquired in November 2008 by Fung Capital Europe, the private investment company of Victor and William Fung, who in turn control the Hong Kong fashion conglomerate of Li & Fung. Founded in 1906 and now a very extensive global trading group dealing in consumer goods, almost two-thirds of its products are clothing or clothing-related with fashion accessories, including sports and travel items. Hardy Amies is one of several world-famous names now associated with its name, and the House at 14 Savile Row is a thriving retail and design centre with the resource of an archive, often utilising the history of the name for exhibitions, under the direction of archivist Austin Mutti-Mewse.

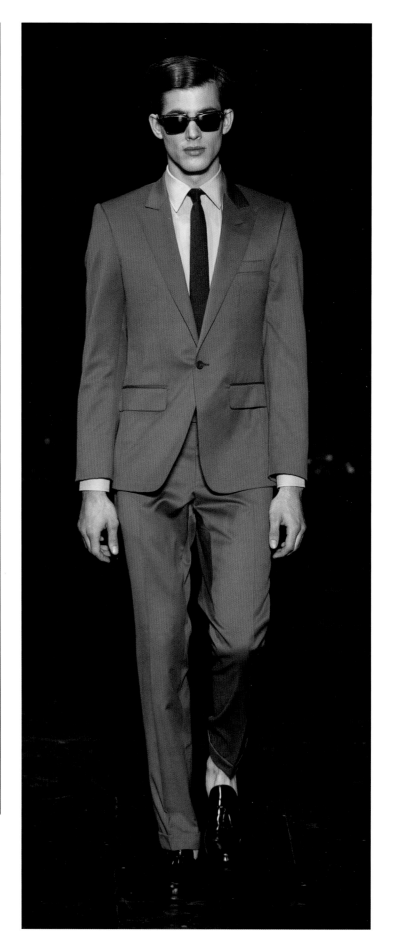

Four of the designs for the spring and summer 2013 collection by Claire Malcolm and her design team, carrying forward the ethics of Hardy Amies which are reflected in the close attention to superb tailoring. The excellent cut results in comfortable clothing with sleek lines, all made of the highest quality materials. These clothes have the timeless quality that Amies sought to capture in his menswear designs and use a colour palette of today.

The Evolution of the Name

Above: *HRH Princess Alexandra, the Hon Lady Ogilvy, with Austin Mutti–Mewse, director of the Hardy Amies Ltd archive. They are examining the bound album compiled at the instigation of Amies and entitled simply 'The Queen', a photographic record of many of the Amies designs worn by HM Queen Elizabeth II from 1951 to the 1990s.*

Opposite page: *The immaculately clad young Hardy Amies in his Savile Row office in 1947. The room was decorated for him by John Fowler and Alexis ffrench. Behind him can be seen a bust bought from his friend Syrie Maugham, with whom he regularly played canasta. The room was soon regarded as an extravagance and re–named the Sheridan Room; it was later used by Neil Roger for his in–house business. Today it forms part of the ground floor showrooms for the current ranges of Hardy Amies menswear. Hardy Amies featured many times in Eleanor Lambert's famous 'Best Dressed Lists', both as designer to notable clients and on his own account, achieving a place in The Hall of Fame in 1974.*

As part of the restructure of the Amies business, the design and manufacture of women's couture ceased, and attention is now concentrated on strengthening the menswear labels worldwide. In 2010 Claire Malcolm was appointed menswear designer at 14 Savile Row and has been responsible, with her design team, for the re–launch of the label based on the history of Hardy Amies and an updating of his own taste and success.

Claire Malcolm graduated from Middlesex University and worked on the 'Kim' label of Kim Jones from 2006. The subsequent collections were shown in New York, London and Paris; she also acted as consultant to various clothing–related companies, including in 2008–09 Kanye West's 'Pastelle' range. Enthused by men's tailoring, she worked with Patrick Grant at Norton & Sons on Savile Row and designed for the revived E. Tautz & Sons label, a British tailor established in 1867, which included Winston Churchill amongst its clients. The new collection won the Best Menswear Award at the 2010 British Fashion Awards.

Her collections for the Hardy Amies label continue to attract favourable press–coverage and to re–assert the contemporary aspects of Amies' own beliefs, as expressed in his menswear collections over the decades and in his *ABC of Men's Fashion*, notably his much–quoted statement: 'A man should look as if he had bought his clothes with intelligence, put them on with care, and then forgotten all about them'.

ACKNOWLEDGEMENTS

With grateful thanks to Her Majesty The Queen for gracious permission to reproduce images and to paraphrase information contained in letters to the late Sir Hardy Amies.

The late Sir Hardy Amies
Geoffrey Angold
The late Murray Arbeid
Ian Askew
Bath Museum of Fashion: Elaine Uttley; Vivien Hynes
The late Count Nicolas van den Branden
Brentwood School: I. Davies: Headmaster; D. Taylor: Second Master; Mrs Christine de Hamel: Librarian; Graham Kiff: Head of Hardy Amies Design Centre
Brighton Museum: Stella Beddoes; Martin Pel
British Airways: Jim Davies of BA Speedbird Centre; Paul Jarvis, Victoria Madden;
Karen Brown
Mrs Margaret Brown
Buckingham Palace: Caroline Baker, the Private Secretary's Office
Stafford Cliff
Alison Constable
Stanley Cox's family
Vincenzina and Barrie Daniels
Roy Dixon
Charles Duff
Mr and Mrs Timothy Fargher
Fortnum & Mason archive: Dr Andrea Tanner
David Freeman
Frederick Fox

Diana Furlonger
Ian Garlant
General Motors archive: Kathleen Adelson
Madeleine Ginsburg
Glyndebourne Opera archive: Joanna Townsend
Derek Granger
Guy Grevett Archive: Mike Hoban
W. Robert Griffiths
Miss Anna Harvey
David Harvey
Miss Julie Harris
Lady Selina Hastings
Giles Hefer
Philip Hewat–Jaboor
IPC Picture Library
Timothy Jones
Stacey Kennedy
Mara McGregor
Manchester Museum, Platt Hall: Miles Lambert
Jon Moore
Museum of London: Beatrice Behlen
Austin Mutti–Mewse
Sir Ronald McIntosh
The staff of the National Archives
Mrs Brenda Naylor
John Owen
Anthony Palliser
Norman Parkinson Archive: Alex Anthony
Kenneth A. Partridge

Michael Raymond
Princess Olga Romanov
Royal Collection Enterprises: Karen Lawson, Picture Library Supervisor
Mrs Edward Ryle–Hodges and family
Mrs Valerie Scobie
Mrs Rollo Seddon
Mrs Valerie Selby
Emmanuel Silverman
Sir Roy Strong
Eiji Takhatake
Mrs Colin Tivey
Mrs Peggy Umpleby
University of Essex: Nigel Cochrane; Holly Ward
University of the Arts, London: Stacey Kennedy, Archivist
Mrs Tugba Unkan
Hugo Vickers
Victoria and Albert Museum: Mark Eastment; Miranda McCaughlin: Victoria and Albert Picture Library
Vogue: Bonnie Robinson
Warner Brothers
Michael York
Tony Yusuf

The staff of Antique Collectors' Club: Diana Steel; Catherine Britton; Tom Conway; Clara Heard; Craig Holden; Ed Munn; Lynn Taylor; James Smith; Kim Yarwood

And to all the many who worked at and for Hardy Amies: although your name may not be here, you are all included in my grateful thanks.

BIBLIOGRAPHY

Amies, Hardy, *Some Clerihews*, Rampant Lion Press, London, 1947
Amies, Hardy, *Just So Far*, Collins, London, 1954
Amies, Hardy, *ABC of Men's Fashion*, Newnes, London, 1964, revised 2007
Amies, Hardy, *Still Here*, Weidenfeld & Nicolson, London, 1984
Amies, Hardy, *The Englishman's Suit*, Quartet Books, London, 1994
Barnes, Alison, *Royal Sisters Volume Three*, Pitkin, London, 1951

Birt, Catherine, *Royal Sisters Volume One*, Pitkin, London, 1949
Bradford, Sarah, *Elizabeth: A Biography of Her Majesty the Queen*, William Heinemann Ltd, London, 1996
Brendon Piers, Whitehead Phillip, *The Windsors: A Dynasty Revealed*, Hodder & Stoughton, London, 1994
Breward Christopher, Conekin Becky, Cox Caroline, *The Englishness of English Dress*, Berg, Oxford, 2002

Breward Christopher, Ehrman Edwina, Evans Caroline, *The London Look: Fashion from Street to Catwalk*, Yale University Press/ Museum of London, 2004
Buckton, Henry, *Artists & Authors at War*, Leo Cooper, London, 1999
Buckton, Henry (ed.), *By Royal Command*, Peter Owen, London, 1997
Carter, Ernestine, *20th Century Fashion*, Eyre Methuen, London, 1975
Carter, Ernestine, *The Changing World of Fashion*, Weidenfeld & Nicolson, London, 1977

Chase Edna Woolman, Chase Ilka, *Always In Vogue*, Gollancz, London, 1954

Clark, Brigadier S. F., *The Royal Tour: Parts One to Four*, Pitkin, London, 1953-1954

Coleman, Elizabeth Ann, *The Genius of Charles James*, the Brooklyn Museum, New York, 1983

Creed, Charles, *Maid to Measure*, Jarrolds, Norwich, 1961

Daily Mail, *Ideal Home Book 1946-47*, London, 1947

Daily Mail, Associated Newspapers Ltd, London, 1996

Daily Mirror, International Publishing Corporation, London, 1968

Decorative Arts Society, The, *Journal number 33*, London, 2009

De Courcy, Anne, *The Last Season*, Phoenix, London, 2003

De Guitaut, Caroline, *The Royal Tour: A Souvenir Album*, Royal Collection Publications, London, 2009

De la Haye, Amy (ed.), *The Cutting Edge: Fifty Years of British Fashion*, V&A Publications, London, 1996

Derrick Robin, Muir Robin (eds.), *Unseen Vogue: The Secret History of Fashion Photography*, Little, Brown & Company, London, 2002

Dior, Christian, *Dior By Dior*, Weidenfeld & Nicolson, London, 1957

Drapers Record, The, EMAP Ltd, London 1938

Eastoe, Jane, *Elizabeth: Reigning In Style*, Pavilion Books, London, 2012

Edwards, Anne & Robb, *The Queen's Clothes*, Elm Tree Books, London, 1977

Eve's Journal, C Arthur Pearson, London, 1939

Evening Standard, The, Associated Newspapers, 1947-1984

ffrench, Yvonne, *Here Lived...A Note on Some Former Tenants of 14 Savile Row*, W. Heffer, Cambridge, 1948

Field, Leslie, *The Queen's Jewels: The Personal Collection of Elizabeth II*, Weidenfeld & Nicolson, London, 1987

Flair, National Magazine Company, 1964

Garland, Madge, *Fashion: A Picture Guide To Its Creators and Creations*, Penguin, London, 1962

Garland, Madge, *The Indecisive Decade*, Macdonald, London, 1968

Gibbings, Sarah, *The Tie*, Studio Editions, London, 1990

Giroud, Francoise, *Dior: Christian Dior 1905-1957*, Thames & Hudson, London, 1987

Globe & Mail, The Globe and Mail Inc, Toronto, Canada, 1947

Glyndebourne Festival Opera Programme Books, 1956-61

Glynn, Prudence, *In Fashion: Dress In the Twentieth Century*, George Allen & Unwin, London, 1978

Harper's Bazaar, National Magazine Company, Hearst Corporation, London, 1935 -2003

Harpers & Queen, National Magazine Company, Hearst Corporation, London, 1970-2003

Hartnell, Norman, *Silver and Gold*, Evans Brothers, London, 1955

House & Garden, Condé Nast Publications, London

Hull Daily Mail, Northcliffe Media Ltd, 1951.

Independent, The, Independent News and Media Ltd, 1995

Journal de Charleroi, Charleroi, 1944

Keenan, Bridget, *The Women We Wanted to Look Like*, Macmillan, London, 1977

King, Viva, *The Weeping and the Laughter*, Macdonald and Janes, London, 1976

Lambert, Angela, *1939: The Last Season of Peace*, Weidenfeld & Nicolson, London, 1989

Lees-Milne Alvilde, Verey Rosemary, *The Englishman's Garden*, Allen Lane, London, 1982

Lees-Milne, James, *Ceaseless Turmoil: Diaries 1988-1992*, John Murray, London, 2004

Lewis, R.R., *The History of Brentwood School*, Brentwood, 1981

Lewis-Crown, Peter, *House of Lachasse: The Story of a Very English Gentleman*, Delancey Press, London, 2009

Lyall, Gavin, The Pictorial Story of *the Royal Tour of India and Pakistan and State Visits to Nepal and Iran*, Pitkins, London, 1961.

Lynn, Olga, *Oggie: The Memoirs of Olga Lynn*, Weidenfeld & Nicholson, London, 1955

MacCarthy, Fiona, *Last Curtsey: the End of the Debutantes*, Faber & Faber, London, 2006

MacLean's, Rogers Media Inc., Toronto, Canada, 1952

Marshall, Francis, *London West*, The Studio, London and New York, 1944

McDowell, Colin, *A Hundred Years of Royal Style*, Muller Blond & White, London, 1985

McDowell, Colin, *The Literary Companion to Fashion*, Sinclair-Stevenson, London, 1995

McDowell, Colin, *Forties Fashion and the New Look*, Bloomsbury, London, 1997

Menkes, Suzy, *The Royal Jewels*, Grafton, London, 1985

Minneapolis Star, The Star Tribune Company, Minnesota USA, 1960

Montreal Daily Star, John Wilson McConnell, Quebec, Canada, 1947-1968

Morais, Richard, *Pierre Cardin: The Man Who Became A Label*, Bantam Press, London, 1991

Muir, Robin, *Norman Parkinson; Portraits In Fashion*, Palazzo Editions, Bath, 2010

Mulvagh, Jane, *Costume Jewellery in Vogue*, Thames & Hudson, London, 1988

Mulvagh, Jane, *Vogue: A History of 20th Century Fashion*, Bloomsbury Books, London, 1988.

Munn, Geoffrey, *Tiaras: A History of Splendour*, Antique Collectors' Club, Woodbridge, 2002

Museum of London, transcripts of interviews with staff members of Hardy Amies Ltd, 1989

New Statesman, The, New Statesman Ltd, London, 1940-1947

News Review, News Journal Company, Delaware, USA, 1940

News, The, Indianapolis, Eugene S. Pulliam, Indianapolis, USA, 1984

New Zealand Herald, APN News and Media, Auckland, New Zealand, 1979

O'Brien-ffrench, Conrad, *Delicate Mission: Autobiography of a Secret Agent*, Skilton and Shaw, London, 1979

Observer, The, Guardian News and Media Ltd., 1939-1980

Packard, Anne, *The Royal Tour of Canada*, Daily Graphic, London, 1951

Palmer, Alexandra, *Dior: A New look. A New Enterprise*, V&A Publishing, London 2009

Palmer, Charles F., *Adventures of a Slum Fighter*, Tupper and Love, USA, 1955

Parkinson, Norman, *Sisters Under The Skin*, Quartet Books, London, 1978

Parkinson, Norman, *Would You Let Your Daughter*, Weidenfeld & Nicolson, London, 1985

Parkinson, Norman, *Lifework*, Octopus Books, London, 1986

Pepper, Terence, *Norman Parkinson*, National Portrait Gallery, London, 1980

Picture Post, Edward G. Hulton, London, 1938-57

Pick, Michael, 'Royal Design, Loyal Style', The London Collections, 1977

Pick, Michael, *Be Dazzled!*, Pointed Leaf Press, New York, 2007

Pimlott, Ben, *The Queen: Elizabeth II and the Monarchy*, Harper Collins, London, 2001

Pringle, Margaret, *Dance Little Ladies: The Days of the Debutante*, Orbis, London, 1977

Quant, Mary, *Quant by Quant*, Cassell, London, 1966

Robinson, Julian, *Fashion In the Forties*, Academy, London, 1976

Ross, Josephine, *Society in Vogue*, Conde Nast Books, London, 1992

Saville, Margaret, *Royal Sisters Volume Two*, Pitkin, London, 1950

Saville, Margaret, *Royal Sisters Volume Five*, Pitkin, London, 1953

Scott, Elizabeth, *Royal Sisters Volume Four*, Pitkin, London, 1952

Seebohm, Caroline, *The Man Who Was Vogue*, Weidenfeld & Nicolson, London, 1982

Seymour, Miranda, *Chaplin's Girl: The Life and Loves of Virginia Cherrill*, Simon & Schuster, London, 2009

Strand Magazine, The, George Newnes, London, 1947

Strong, Roy, *Cecil Beaton: The Royal Portraits*, Thames & Hudson, London, 1998

Sunday Chronicle, Edward G. Hulton, Manchester, 1952

Sunday Times, The, London, 1961

Sydney Sun, Sydney, Australia, 1965

Tailor & Cutter, The, 1949

Talbot, Godfrey, *The Royal Family*, Country Life Books, Surrey, 1980

Tatler, The, Illustrated Newspapers, 1951

Thaarup, Aage, *Heads and Tails*, Cassell, London, 1956

The Queen, Jocelyn Stevens, 1945-60

Time, Time Inc., 1951

Times, The, London, Times Newspapers Ltd, 2010

Vaughan-Thomas, Wynford, *Royal Tour: 1953-1954*, Hutchinson, London, 1954

Vickers, Hugo, *Cecil Beaton: The Authorised Biography*, Weidenfeld & Nicolson, London, 1985

Vogue, Conde Nast Publications , London, 1935-2003

Watt, Judith, *The Penguin Book of Twentieth Century Fashion Writing*, Viking, London, 1999

Wilcox Claire, Mendes Valerie, *Modern Fashion In Detail*, V&A Museum, 1991

Withers, Audrey, *LifeSpan*, Peter Owen, London, 1994

Wolters John, Stephenson Kerry, *The Best Of Days? Memories of Brentwood School*, Brentwood School, 1999

Woman, IPC Magazines, London, 1951

Women's Wear Daily, Fairchild Publications, 1935-85

Wood, Martin, *John Fowler: Prince of Decorators*, Frances Lincoln Ltd., London, 2007

York, Pat, *Going Strong*, Arcade Publishing, New York, 1991

Young, Sheila, *The Queen's Jewellery*, Ebury Press, London, 1969

Yoxall, H. W., *A Fashion of Life*, William Heinemann Ltd, London, 1966

INDEX

Numbers in *italic* type denote images

AUTHOR'S BIOGRAPHY

Michael Pick is a London-based fine arts and design consultant. He was a director of Stair & Company Ltd (London and New York) and Partridge Fine Arts plc. A Fellow of the Royal Society of Arts and formerly an Exhibitioner in History of Gonville and Caius College, Cambridge, he is the author of seven books on design and the decorative arts, on which he has lectured and written extensively in the UK, overseas, and on board Queen Mary 2. He has contributed to numerous publications, including *The Times, The Daily Telegraph, The Independent, Apollo, The Connoisseur, Antiques, The Antique Collector, Tatler, Harpers & Queen*, and *Vogue*. A founder Committee Member of the Twentieth Century Society, the officially recognised British post-1900s architectural preservation group, one of his subsequent commissions was for the complete renovation of the Norman Hartnell Mayfair building with its *art-moderne* interiors. He wrote *BE DAZZLED! The Life of Norman Hartnell*, about whom he has lectured at the Victoria & Albert Museum and at the Chichester and Oxford Literary Festivals. In the late 1970s and 1980s he worked freelance with fashion PR Percy Savage and has also broadcast on television in the UK and abroad. *Hardy Amies* is the direct result of Sir Hardy Amies' own suggestion that he write such a book, and it draws on the author's conversations with him.

PICTURE CREDITS

All pictures are taken from the Hardy Amies Ltd Archive and the Hardy Amies Langford Archive, unless specified otherwise. Every effort has been made to secure permission to reproduce the images contained within this book, and we are grateful to the individuals and institutions that have assisted in this task. Any errors or omissions are entirely unintentional and the details should be addressed to the publisher.

Front cover: Hardy Amies Ltd Archive, circa 1965
Back cover: June Clarke, Fiona Campbell–Walker and Hardy Amies, 1953 © Norman Parkinson Ltd/courtesy Norman Parkinson Archive
Endpapers: an original Advent/Christmas greetings card depicting 14 Savile Row, from the Hardy Amies Ltd Archive
Title page facing: Hardy Amies in his eighties © Norman Parkinson Ltd/courtesy Norman Parkinson Archive
Title page: the current Hardy Amies logo as a flag outside 14 Savile Row, image courtesy Hardy Amies Ltd
Foreword: Marc cartoon commissioned by Hardy Amies and used as a Christmas card, circa 1978. Hardy Amies Langford Archive
Photograph of Michael York in Cornwall taken by Pat York © reproduced by kind permission
Introduction: Portrait of Sir Hardy Amies by Anthony Palliser, 1994, now hanging in the Hardy Amies Design Centre, Brentwood School, Essex, (reproduced by kind permission of the artist)

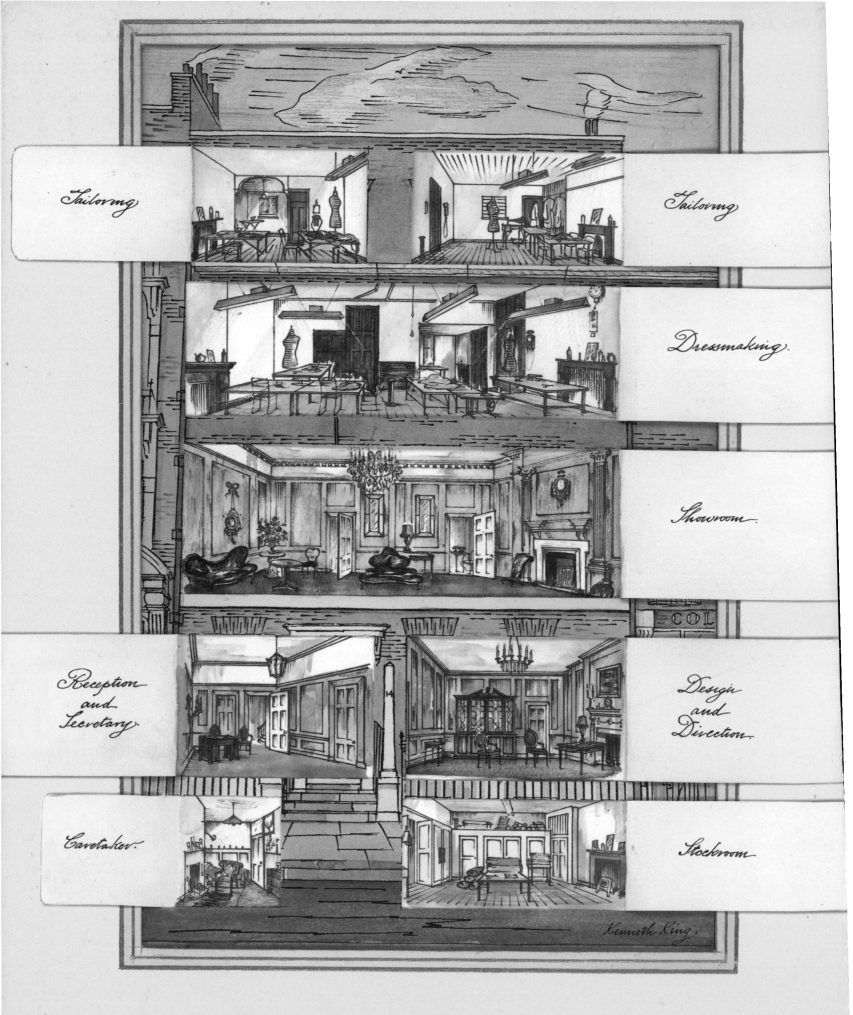

Tailoring

Tailoring

Dressmaking.

Showroom.

Reception
and
Secretary.

Design
and
Direction.

Caretaker.

Stockroom

Kenneth King.

Hardy Amies Ltd,
14 Savile Row,
London.
W.1.